The
Mohawk

Indians
of North
America

Heritage Edition

Indians
of North
America

Heritage Edition

◀ Indians ▶
of North
◀ America ▶

The Mohawk

Nancy Bonvillain

Foreword by
Ada E. Deer
University of Wisconsin-Madison

CHELSEA HOUSE
PUBLISHERS
A Haights Cross Communications ✈ Company

Philadelphia

COVER: By the late 1800s, the Mohawks were renowned for crafting fancy baskets like this one, which they sold at tourist destinations such as Saratoga Springs and Niagara Falls, New York.

CHELSEA HOUSE PUBLISHERS

VP, NEW PRODUCT DEVELOPMENT Sally Cheney
DIRECTOR OF PRODUCTION Kim Shinners
CREATIVE MANAGER Takeshi Takahashi
MANUFACTURING MANAGER Diann Grasse

Staff for THE MOHAWK

EXECUTIVE EDITOR Lee Marcott
EDITOR Christian Green
PRODUCTION EDITOR Noelle Nardone
PHOTO EDITOR Sarah Bloom
SERIES AND COVER DESIGNER Keith Trego
LAYOUT 21st Century Publishing and Communications, Inc.

First Printing

9 8 7 6 5 4 3 2 1

Library of Congress Cataloging-in-Publication Data

Bonvillain, Nancy.
   The Mohawk / Nancy Bonvillain.
      p. cm.—(Indians of North America, revised)
Includes bibliographical references and index.
   ISBN 0-7910-7991-0 — ISBN 0-7910-8352-7(pbk.)
   1. Mohawk Indians. I. Title. II. Series.
E99.M8.B66 2004
974.7004'975542—dc22

                                                2004004714

Contents

Foreword

Ada E. Deer

American Indians are an integral part of our nation's life and history. Yet most Americans think of their Indian neighbors as stereotypes; they are woefully uninformed about them as fellow humans. They know little about the history, culture, and contributions of Native people. In this new millennium, it is essential for every American to know, understand, and share in our common heritage. The Cherokee teacher, the Mohawk steelworker, and the Ojibwe writer all express their tribal heritage while living in mainstream America.

The revised INDIANS OF NORTH AMERICA series, which focuses on some of the continent's larger tribes, provides the reader with an accurate perspective that will better equip him/her to live and work in today's world. Each tribe has a unique history and culture, and knowledge of individual tribes is essential to understanding the Indian experience.

Prior to the arrival of Columbus in 1492, scholars estimate the Native population north of the Rio Grande ranged from seven to twenty-five million people who spoke more than three hundred different languages. It has been estimated that ninety percent of the Native population was wiped out by disease, war, relocation, and starvation. Today there are more than 567 tribes, which have a total population of more than two million. When Columbus arrived in the Bahamas, the Arawak Indians greeted him with gifts, friendship, and hospitality. He noted their ignorance of guns and swords and wrote they could easily be overtaken with fifty men and made to do whatever he wished. This unresolved clash in perspectives continues to this day.

A holistic view recognizing the connections of all people, the land, and animals pervades the life and thinking of Native people. These core values—respect for each other and all living things; honoring the elders; caring, sharing, and living in balance with nature; and using not abusing the land and its resources—have sustained Native people for thousands of years.

American Indians are recognized in the U.S. Constitution. They are the only group in this country who has a distinctive *political* relationship with the federal government. This relationship is based on the U.S. Constitution, treaties, court decisions, and attorney-general opinions. Through the treaty process, millions of acres of land were ceded *to* the U.S. government *by* the tribes. In return, the United States agreed to provide protection, health care, education, and other services. All 377 treaties were broken by the United States. Yet treaties are the supreme law of the land as stated in the U.S. Constitution and are still valid. Treaties made more than one hundred years ago uphold tribal rights to hunt, fish, and gather.

Since 1778, when the first treaty was signed with the Lenni-Lenape, tribal sovereignty has been recognized and a government-to-government relationship was established. This concept of tribal power and authority has continuously been misunderstood by the general public and undermined by the states. In a series of court decisions in the 1830s, Chief Justice John Marshall described tribes as "domestic dependent nations." This status is not easily understood by most people and is rejected by state governments who often ignore and/or challenge tribal sovereignty. Sadly, many individual Indians and tribal governments do not understand the powers and limitations of tribal sovereignty. An overarching fact is that Congress has plenary, or absolute, power over Indians and can exercise this sweeping power at any time. Thus, sovereignty is tenuous.

Since the July 8, 1970, message President Richard Nixon issued to Congress in which he emphasized "self-determination without termination," tribes have re-emerged and have utilized the opportunities presented by the passage of major legislation such as the American Indian Tribal College Act (1971), Indian Education Act (1972), Indian Education and Self-Determination Act (1975), American Indian Health Care Improvement Act (1976), Indian Child Welfare Act (1978), American Indian Religious Freedom Act (1978), Indian Gaming Regulatory Act (1988), and Native American Graves Preservation and Repatriation Act (1990). Each of these laws has enabled tribes to exercise many facets of their sovereignty and consequently has resulted in many clashes and controversies with the states and the general public. However, tribes now have more access to and can afford attorneys to protect their rights and assets.

Under provisions of these laws, many Indian tribes reclaimed power over their children's education with the establishment of tribal schools and thirty-one tribal colleges. Many Indian children have been rescued from the foster-care system. More tribal people are freely practicing their traditional religions. Tribes with gaming revenue have raised their standard of living with improved housing, schools, health clinics, and other benefits. Ancestors' bones have been reclaimed and properly buried. All of these laws affect and involve the federal, state, and local governments as well as individual citizens.

Tribes are no longer people of the past. They are major players in today's economic and political arenas; contributing millions of dollars to the states under the gaming compacts and supporting political candidates. Each of the tribes in INDIANS OF NORTH AMERICA demonstrates remarkable endurance, strength, and adaptability. They are buying land, teaching their language and culture, and creating and expanding their economic base, while developing their people and making decisions for future generations. Tribes will continue to exist, survive, and thrive.

Ada E. Deer
University of Wisconsin-Madison
June 2004

1

Ancestors

I n 1644, a Dutch minister named Johannes Megapolensis visited Mohawk territory and made the following observations:

> The land is good, and fruitful in everything which supplies human needs. The country is very mountainous, partly soil, partly rocks, and with elevations so exceeding high that they appear to almost touch the clouds. Thereon grow the finest fir trees the eye ever saw. There are also in this country oaks, alders, beeches, elms, willows, etc. In the forests, and here and there along the water side, and on the islands, there grows an abundance of chestnuts, plums, hazel nuts, large walnuts of several sorts. The ground on the hills is covered with bushes of blueberries; the ground in the flat land near the rivers is covered with strawberries, which grow here so plentifully in the fields, that one can lie down and eat them. Grapevines also grow here naturally in great abundance along the

roads, paths and creeks. I have seen whole pieces of land where vine stood by vine and grew very luxuriantly, climbing to the top of the largest and loftiest trees. In the forests is great plenty of deer. There are also many partridges, heath-hens and pigeons that fly together in thousands, and a great number of all kinds of fowl, swans, geese, ducks which sport upon the river in thousands. Beside the deer and elks, there are panthers, bears, wolves, and foxes. In the river is a great plenty of all kinds of fish—pike, eels, perch, lampreys, cat fish, sun fish, shad, bass, and sturgeon.

In this bountiful environment lived the Mohawk. This powerful *nation* once decided the fortunes of many peoples—Indian and non-Indian alike—in what is now the United States and Canada.

The Mohawks whom Megapolensis visited in the seventeenth century were descendants of peoples who in ancient times had lived in present-day New York State. Beginning approximately ten thousand years ago, northeastern North America was inhabited by men and women who subsisted by hunting animals and gathering wild plants, fruits, and nuts. Gradually, over many thousands of years, they developed sophisticated tools and utensils, and refined such arts as pottery making and basketry.

In order to survive, these prehistoric people had to move frequently, following the animals they hunted and searching out new sources of wild plants and fruits. They dealt with the hardships they encountered by living in small groups and offering each other assistance and companionship.

It is impossible to fix exact dates for the arrival of ancestors of the modern Mohawks in the Northeast, but they probably migrated from areas to the west sometime between 1700 B.C. and 1200 B.C. After that time, three major periods of cultural development occurred in the Northeast—the Early Woodland period, the Middle Woodland period, and the Late

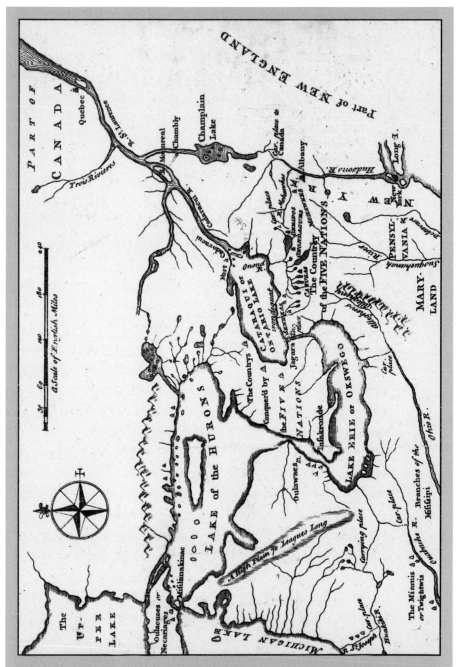

This map, c. 1650, shows the land held by the five nations of the Iroquois, which included the Mohawk, Seneca, Cayuga, Onondaga, and Oneida. The Mohawk Nation settled in the area of the Mohawk River valley, west of what is now Albany, New York.

Woodland period. These stages can be identified by continuities or changes in people's foods, housing, methods of making tools and utensils, and styles of decorating pottery and other equipment. (For additional information on this era of cultural development, enter "Woodland period" into any search engine and browse the many sites listed.)

One of the first types of societies (or traditions) associated with the ancestors of the Mohawks is called Meadowood. This tradition existed around 1000 B.C., during the Early Woodland phase in central New York State. Although people in those times were nomadic, following their animal prey, they maintained a central base area where they lived between hunting and fishing expeditions.

Objects have been found at Meadowood sites that were not of local origin. Among these items were conch shells from the Gulf of Mexico, copper from Lake Superior, silver from Ontario, mica (a mineral) from the southern Appalachian Mountains, and grizzly bear teeth from the Rocky Mountains. These discoveries indicate that prehistoric peoples had long-distance trading networks through which they exchanged local goods for valuables from regions thousands of miles away. The existence of trade items also proves that people did not live in total isolation from one another but established friendly contacts with their neighbors.

Cultures like those of Meadowood continued for hundreds of years. Then in the Middle Woodland period, significant changes in the Indians' way of life took place. By around A.D. 200, settlement patterns had changed. People constructed larger villages that were relocated every few years, apparently to bring them closer to food sources. The people's houses, made of bark and earth, could be rebuilt in a relatively short time but were spacious enough to accommodate several families.

Middle Woodland villages were located near rivers, giving residents easy access to travel routes. The typical mode of transportation was by canoe in rivers and lakes, for traveling on foot through the region's dense forests was slow and difficult.

Middle Woodland peoples relied on a great variety of wild foods, including animals such as deer and bear, many species of fish, and different kinds of nuts, berries, and plants. Through trade they were able to acquire goods, including smoking pipes manufactured from stone originating in other parts of North America and pendants made from stone and shark's teeth. These people also possessed copper and shell beads that they presumably used to decorate clothing and other objects.

A typical Middle Woodland village, settled in about A.D. 800 to 900, was Hunter's Home, situated on the Mohawk River near present-day Schenectady, New York. People at Hunter's Home had begun to grow some of their own food. Even though seeds or crops have not been found, the discovery at the site of mortars and pestles—utensils used for grinding seeds and corn kernels—indicates that people there must have grown corn.

Over time, the Indians of the Northeast came to rely more and more on farming for their food supply. The people of Central America, who had learned to cultivate crops long before, probably contributed indirectly to the Woodland Indians' knowledge of farming techniques. Just as Woodland peoples traded for raw materials, utensils, and beads, they also exchanged ideas. Over hundreds of years, the innovations of one Indian group could be transmitted to peoples thousands of miles away.

Farming was advantageous because it gave people a secure source of food. But Middle Woodland people did not abandon their old ways completely. They continued to gather wild plants, fruits, and nuts and to fish and hunt in the forests. A greater variety and abundance of food led to larger and more permanent villages. Middle Woodland peoples began to alter their settlement patterns in different seasons. During the spring and summer, when foods were plentiful, they lived in large villages. They split up into smaller groups after harvests in autumn and winter, when plants and animals became scarce.

The Late Woodland period began approximately A.D. 1000. A major cultural phase of this period was the Owasco tradition, which lasted from A.D. 1000 to 1300. Many cultural changes were adopted during this time.

In the Owasco phase, people shifted their villages from river sites to hilltops. Although no one knows for certain why this was done, Owasco peoples probably sought safety on hills from their enemies. In addition to protection given by hilltop locations, people surrounded their villages with palisades—walls of long poles spaced a few feet apart that made it difficult for intruders to enter their villages undetected. Some settlements were protected further by ditches dug outside the palisades and by earthen barricades built inside. Villagers would probably have created such elaborate structures only if they were afraid of being attacked. Although it is unknown who their enemies were or what caused the warfare, they may have fought with neighboring peoples for control of valuable farmland.

Owasco villages gradually became larger and more concentrated. The small, dispersed settlements of earlier times were abandoned because it was easier to protect a few concentrated areas than numerous isolated locales. Oblong houses covered with elm bark were typical Owasco dwellings. Several families lived in each house. They subsisted on the crops they grew, supplemented by wild plants and animals. Corn was their most important crop. Several varieties of beans and squash were also produced.

The final cultural phase within the Late Woodland period began around A.D. 1300 and is called the *Iroquoian* tradition. The term Iroquoian is used to describe a group who spoke related languages and had similar economic systems, social customs, and religious beliefs. The Iroquoians emerged from earlier Owasco societies, retaining the same basic way of life but developing and furthering certain elements of their culture.

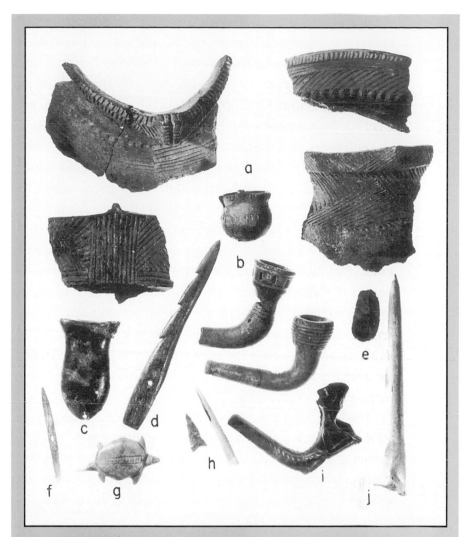

Late Iroquoian artifacts: (a, b) pottery fragments; (c) stone pipe bowl; (d) deer antler harpoon; (e) stone scraper (f) needle used to sew nets; (g) stone tortoise amulet; (h) stone and bone arrowheads; (i) pottery pipes; (j) dagger made from a human bone.

Early Iroquoian villages have been excavated near present-day Albany, Kingston, and New Paltz, New York. These villages were relatively permanent and were relocated every ten or twenty years to a distance of perhaps two or three miles. Trails, some of which still exist, connected villages to frequently used hunting and fishing stations. Meat and fish were supplemented by crops, including corn, beans, squash, melons, and sunflowers.

Iroquoian residences were large, rectangular structures made of wooden poles covered with elm bark. These *longhouses* had doors located at each end. Inside there was a central row of hearths for cooking and heating. A hearth was shared by two families, each having separate living quarters. Longhouses usually accommodated as many as ten families. (For additional information on these structures, enter "Iroquois longhouses" into any search engine and browse the many sites listed.)

Iroquoian peoples built ever-thicker and sturdier palisades around their villages, which suggests an increase in warfare. They often erected two or three rows of poles rather than the single rows that had been built in earlier times. As settlements became more concentrated and as warfare increased, long-distance trade diminished. Few materials originating in faraway places have been found at Iroquoian sites, suggesting that individual groups had become more self-sufficient.

Geographic separation eventually led distinct groups to form among the Iroquoians. They soon became divided into several nations, each with its own name. One such nation was the Kanienkehaka (ga-nyen-ge-HA-ga), meaning "People of the Place of Flint." These people, known to non-Indians as the Mohawks, would play a dramatic role in the history of North America.

2

People of the Place of Flint

For centuries, the Kanienkehaka, or the Mohawks, lived in the Mohawk River valley west of what is now Albany, New York. Their hunting territories extended northward into the Adirondack Mountains and southward along the Susquehanna River to present-day Oneonta, New York. To the west were other Iroquoian nations, including the Oneida, the Onondaga, the Cayuga, and the Seneca. They spoke closely related languages and developed very similar cultures. East of the Mohawk were the Mahican, the Housatonic, and the Wappinger Nations. Linked by similar languages and cultures, these groups are known as *Algonkians*. The ways of life of the Iroquoians and the Algonkians were quite different—a situation that sometimes led to conflicts between the two groups.

At the beginning of their recorded history (approximately A.D. 1500), the Mohawks continued the traditions developed by their Iroquoian ancestors. The Mohawk people lived in three large villages, all located on the south side of the Mohawk River in the heart of the nation's territory. One village, named Tionontoguen (de-yo-non-DO-gen), meaning "valley" or "between two mountains," was referred to as the center or capital. These three villages, as well as several smaller ones, were relocated from time to time, probably every ten or twenty years, when the nutrients in nearby soil had been exhausted and the fields became infertile.

The Mohawks lived in large longhouses made of wooden poles covered with earth and elm bark. These longhouses were usually about twenty-five feet wide and averaged eighty feet in length, although some were as long as two hundred feet. A house typically contained a central row of four or five hearths, each accommodating two families of perhaps five or six people. Platforms built along the inner walls, about one foot from the ground, were covered with reed mats or animal pelts and used for seating during the day and sleeping at night. People stored utensils, tools, and food on shelves along the wall. Large bins made of bark were placed between each family's quarters within the longhouse. These bins were used to store corn, dried fruit, and cured deer meat. At the ends of houses, people kept firewood, which they used for both cooking and heating.

Villages were located on hilltops close to the lakes and rivers that provided the major routes of travel. The Mohawks selected their sites near drinking water as well. Small villages contained about thirty longhouses but larger ones held as many as one hundred. The people built wooden palisades around their villages for protection against enemy attacks. Planting fields lay outside the boundaries of residential settlements.

Women provided their families with foods from farming. They planted seeds in the spring, weeded fields throughout the summer, and harvested crops in the fall. They used wooden hoes to dig holes for seeds, which they planted in small mounds of earth. Women prepared seeds before planting by soaking

Mohawks resided in longhouses, which were made of wooden poles covered with earth and elm bark. Inside there was a central row of hearths for cooking and heating and they usually accommodated as many as ten families.

them in medicinal solutions for several days. They believed that this procedure kept crows away from their crops. They planted many varieties of corn and had numerous recipes for its preparation. Corn kernels were typically dried in the sun and baked into breads. Women also prepared corn soups, often adding berries, meat, or fish for flavor.

The relationship between women and food production is symbolized by the belief that a female deity in the ancient past gave corn, beans, and squash to the people. These primary crops are referred to as either the Three Sisters or Our Life Supporters.

Because women performed the farm work, they were considered the owners of their family's fields and produce. Females controlled the distribution of all food within their households. Prominent women also dictated what land could be used by each member of their family.

Women gathered fruits, nuts, and wild potatoes. Strawberries and blueberries were spread in bark trays and dried in the sun for later use. The Mohawk diet also included hickory nuts, walnuts, acorns, and sunflower seeds. Oils from nuts and seeds were used in cooking. In the early spring, women extracted sap from maple trees, which they used to sweeten tea and dishes made from corn.

Men made important contributions to their families' sustenance, providing fish, wild fowl, and animal meat. They hunted deer, elk, moose, bear, beaver, partridge, and wild turkey. Bows and arrows were the basic hunting gear, although men also used wooden traps to capture deer, and spears and nets to catch birds and fish. Sometimes men and women organized communal deer hunts, during which they could catch as many as one hundred animals. During such hunts, the party walked through the woods in two lines forming a V. The hunters shook rattles and made noises to frighten deer and lead them into the narrow space between the two lines. Once trapped inside the V's point, the animals could be easily killed.

In addition to the variety of foods they consumed, the Mohawks brewed several types of tea. Some were made from hemlock boughs boiled in water and flavored with maple syrup. Others were brewed from wild spices or sassafras root. Teas were also made from numerous herbs and roots that were known to have medicinal value. Herbal teas were part of the treatment for various ailments. In fact, the people had a great deal of medical knowledge. They learned the healing properties of many plants, tree barks, and oils from fish, snakes, and other animals.

Mohawk women made clothing from deerskin, which they dyed black. In rainy or cold weather, people covered themselves with extra pelts. Footwear consisted of moccasins in most seasons, although in the summer the Mohawks wore slippers made from twined cornhusks. They also donned armbands, wristbands, and deerskin belts, which were often decorated with embroidery. Warriors tattooed their body (especially their chest and shoulders) and face. They favored geometric designs and representations of animals.

Strings or belts of *wampum* had great ritual value to the Mohawks. Wampum was made from clam shells and was obtained through trade with Indians on Long Island and in coastal New Jersey. The shells were cut into pieces and made into small beads that were strung together or woven into belts. Different patterns formed by the white and purple beads conveyed different messages. Wampum was given to participants on many significant occasions, such as funerals. It was also used to commemorate important events, such as visits by prominent guests and the conclusion of treaties with other nations. An account of a specific event was "talked into the wampum" and thereby preserved forever.

The Mohawks enjoyed a variety of games, which were often accompanied by betting on individual contestants or teams. One such sport was a ball game, played by two teams of six or eight men. The object of the game was to carry a small deerskin ball through one of two gates erected at either end of a playing field. The players moved the ball using long sticks with a small net at one end. Participants attempted to intercept members of the opposite team in order to make them drop the ball or block them from catching it. Before

The Wampum Bird

White and purple beads called wampum played an important role in traditional Mohawk society. Weaving these beads into belts, the Mohawks formed colorful patterns that functioned to record and commemorate special events. Wampum belts were often presented as gifts to cement alliances with other peoples.

In his 1976 book, Tales of the Iroquois, *a Mohawk Indian named Tehanetorens recorded the following legend about wampum's meaning to his tribe.*

Long ago, a war party of Mohawks captured a young man of the Wampanoag Nation. For some years, the Mohawks had been at war with these people. The captive boy was allowed to live, and was given permission to move freely about the Mohawk Village. He was closely watched so that he might not escape back to the Wampanoag Country.

One day, a young Mohawk hunter came running into the village. He was filled with excitement, for he had seen a strange bird in the forest. This bird was covered with wampum beads. Immediately, a hunting party was organized, and the hunters set out to try and capture this wonderful bird. The bird was as the hunter had described it—covered with white and purple feathers. All of the hunters tried to hit the bird with their arrows. Occasionally, the bird was hit by an arrow, and off would fly a shower of wampum. New wampum appeared on the bird to take the place of the fallen wampum. Finally, after trying to hit the bird for some time, the best hunters began to get discouraged, and one by one, they gave up trying to get the bird.

The young Wampanoag captive, from the unfriendly nation, asked the chief if he could try his luck. The Mohawk warriors did not want this to happen, and even threatened the boy's life. The chief interferred [sic], and told the boy that he could try. "If warriors have tried and failed, surely a mere boy cannot bring down the bird," said the chief.

The warriors finally agreed, and the boy lifted his bow and fitted an arrow. The swift arrow pierced the heart of the bird, and it fell to the earth. Its wampum plumage enriched the people. The boy married the chief's daughter, and with the marriage came peace between the two nations. The boy said, "Wampum shall bring and bind peace and it shall take the place of blood."

a game started, players decided how many successful goals—generally five to eight—would constitute a victory. This ancient Iroquoian game was a precursor of the modern game of lacrosse.

During winter months, people enjoyed a game called snow snakes. A snow snake was a pole, perhaps five to seven feet long, made of polished hickory wood. It measured approximately one inch wide at its head and gradually narrowed to half that width at the bottom. A snow snake was thrown so that it slid very fast along packed snow. The object of the game was to make the snow snake travel the farthest distance.

The lives of the Mohawks were organized around a yearly cycle of activities, based on the phases of the moon. The pivotal division of a year was called Midwinter. It occurred five nights following the appearance of a new moon after the winter solstice (about December 22). The first economic activity took place two moons after Midwinter, when women went into the woods to obtain sap from maple trees. Next, the men went out to hunt the birds that arrived every spring from the south. The men also caught fish, which filled rivers and lakes in enormous numbers.

Next, women began their farming activities. These tasks occupied the summer and fall, ending with annual harvests. In autumn, men left their villages on hunting expeditions. They returned home by the time of the winter solstice, and everyone prepared again for Midwinter and a renewal of the yearly cycle.

Mohawk families were related on the basis of descent through women. This kinship system, called *matrilineal* (from *matri* meaning "mother" and *lineal* meaning "line" or "descent"), linked generations from mother to daughter. The whole society was divided into three clans. A *clan* is a group of people who consider themselves related and often share stories or myths about their common ancestry. Mohawk clans were named after animals—the bear, the wolf, and the turtle. A person automatically belonged to their mother's clan. Since social rules dictated that two people of the same clan could not marry each other, the clan system linked kinship groups to others through marriage.

Clans controlled and distributed farmland to their members. They also owned the longhouses that were inhabited by families related through clan membership. Typically, a household was headed by an elder woman and included her daughters, and the younger women's husbands and children. Sons resided with their mothers until they married. They then moved into their wives' houses.

Marriages were marked with a simple ceremony. Accompanied by her mother and some female relatives and friends, the bride-to-be traveled to the house of her intended husband. When she arrived, she gave a present of corn bread to her future mother-in-law, who returned the honor with a gift of deer meat. Afterward, all in attendance shared in a feast.

The exchange of foods had symbolic meaning. A woman's family offered corn, which was associated with female labor. A man's family reciprocated with deer meat, associated with male labor. Together these gifts represented the interdependence of women and men in the economic well-being of families.

A marriage ideally lasted until the death of one spouse. But if a wife and husband became unhappy with one another, they were free to divorce and seek new mates. However, the couple's mothers frequently tried to mediate disputes and reach a reconciliation.

Women were often referred to as "mothers of the nation," in recognition of the value of their role in the continuity of generations. Another symbolic expression of this occurred in cases of murder. According to Mohawk custom, a murderer's family had to present strings or belts of wampum to the victim's family to atone for the crime. Fines were set at twenty belts for a woman's death and ten for a man's. The double value of a woman's life was deemed appropriate because it reflected not only the loss of her own life but also the lives of the children she might have borne.

The Mohawk Nation was divided into two sections, or moieties. A *moiety* (from the French word for half) is a grouping of clans. The Wolf and Turtle clans formed one moiety, the Bear clan constituted the other. Moieties served certain ceremonial functions, one of which was to prepare and conduct funerals for members of the other group. For instance, when a person belonging to the Wolf clan died, Bear clan people arranged the deceased's funeral ceremony. This custom arose because the Mohawks believed that members of the deceased's clan or moiety were too overcome by grief to be able to conduct a proper rite.

The Mohawks believed in a religion that saw life forces in many forms, such as in animals, natural phenomena, and some special objects. These entities all had power, called *orenda* (o-REN-da). Any animal, object, or force that had orenda was capable of affecting humans. For this reason, people had to treat all entities with care and respect. Because spirit beings gave good things to people, the Mohawks believed that they were obliged to honor the spirit world.

Even though orenda ultimately came from the supernatural realm, people could make use of it to ensure their health and good fortune. Certain people had special abilities to use powers for the benefit of others. These people conducted rituals for individual and community well-being.

The fulfillment of one's dreams was also considered necessary to achieve and maintain health and success. According to the Mohawks' beliefs, dreams were expressions of a person's innermost thoughts and desires. The Mohawks thought that illness could be caused by thwarting the desires expressed in one's dreams. They believed, therefore, that in order to remain healthy or be cured from illness, all people needed to fulfill their dreams' wishes. The desires expressed in some dreams were obvious. For example, if a person dreamed of visiting someone or receiving a particular object, she or he satisfied the desire by making the visit or requesting the item seen in the dream. However, the messages in some dreams were more difficult to interpret. In these cases, the dreamers consulted people who had special powers to interpret a dream's hidden or symbolic meanings. All community members were obliged to help a dreamer fulfill her or his wish. This practice emphasized the interdependence and mutual aid binding people together.

Some illnesses, though, were not related to one's dreams but rather to actions of witches. Witches were believed to be

A Curing Ritual

Harmen van den Bogaert, a Dutch visitor to Mohawk territory, recorded the following account of a curing ritual he witnessed in 1635.

I saw a dozen men together who were going to drive off the devil. The floor of [the] house was thickly covered with the bark of trees for the hunters of the devil to walk upon. They were mostly old men, and they had their faces all painted with red paint—which they always do when they are going to do anything unusual. In the middle of the house they then put a man who was very sick. Close by sat an old woman with a turtle shell in her hands. In the turtle shell were a good many beads. She kept clinking all the while, and all of them sang to the measure; then they would proceed to catch the devil and trample him to death; they trampled the bark to atoms so that none of it remained whole; they beat at it in great amazement and then they blew that dust at one another; and after long stamping and running one of them went to the sick man and took away an otter that he had in his hands; and [one curer] sucked the sick man for awhile in his neck and on the back, and after that he spat in the otter's mouth and threw it down. Then they commenced to throw fire and eat fire, and kept scattering hot ashes and red-hot coal in such a way that I ran out of the house.

jealous or angry men and women who inflicted harm on others. They had several methods of causing sickness or death. They might secretly put dangerous concoctions into a victim's food or drink; or they might use rituals and prayers to carry out their intentions. The Mohawks also believed that witches had the power to transform themselves into animals so that they could wander near their victims without arousing suspicion.

The Mohawks celebrated many kinds of rituals, including seasonal ceremonies concerned with foods and crops, curing ceremonies, and death rites. Seasonal ceremonies occurred in a specific sequence, following a yearly cycle or calendar: The timing and planning of calendrics was organized by Keepers of the Faith, a group of men and women who were among the most respected people in the community.

Each calendric ceremony was composed of several separate rites. The first rite in all ceremonials was a thanksgiving speech offered to supernatural and natural beings and forces. These entities were mentioned and thanked in a special order. Things closest to the earth, such as plants and animals, were noted first. Celestial entities, such as the wind, the sun, and the stars, were mentioned next. The list ended with supernatural beings and the Creator.

After the recitation of thanksgiving, tobacco was sprinkled on a fire as an invocation to spirits. The Mohawks believed that smoke from burning tobacco carried messages to the supernatural realm. Next, a group of rituals associated with each specific ceremonial was performed. At the end of the ceremonial, thanksgivings again were offered to supernatural and natural beings, followed by a communal feast, which often focused on the particular food associated with the occasion.

The first ceremonial of the year was Midwinter, which marked both the end of one year and the beginning of the next. Midwinter was the longest and most complex Mohawk ceremonial. It incorporated elements of thanksgiving, renewal, rejoicing, and preparation for the cycle of natural occurrences and human activities.

Midwinter lasted for nine days, each of which was devoted to performing certain rites. In the initial rite, a pure white dog was ritually strangled and burned. Like tobacco smoke, smoke from the burning dog carcass was thought to carry people's messages to spirits. Because dogs are loyal to their human owners, the animal symbolized the Mohawks' own loyalty to supernatural beings. After the "white dog sacrifice," messengers called Our Uncles went through each house in the village to announce the start of Midwinter. While inside, a messenger took a large wooden paddle and stirred the ashes in every hearth. This rite represented the renewal of the community and the awakening of life forces for the coming year.

After this beginning, several days were devoted to interpreting and fulfilling individual dreams. People went from house to house asking others to guess their dreams by interpreting hints or riddles provided by the dreamer. Each guesser offered an item that she or he believed was seen in the dream. When someone presented the correct object, the dreamer kept the item and returned all others to their original owners. The Mohawks' dream-guessing rituals were lively and entertaining. They released the tension and boredom that often set in during the long, cold winter.

The next section of Midwinter consisted of the Four Sacred Rituals. These included a Feather Dance, Thanksgiving Dance, Personal Chants, and a Bowl Game. To conclude Midwinter, the people performed dances for Our Life Supporters, offering thanks to the spirits of corn, beans, and squash, on whom the Mohawks depended for their survival.

Other calendric ceremonies also concentrated on events in the annual cycle. Their sequence was timed to changes in the natural environment or to people's economic activities. The Mohawks performed ceremonies dedicated to the sun and thunder, which provide warmth and rain to make plants grow.

Other calendric rites were focused on the crops that the Mohawks produced. The rites were performed in the following order each year:

MAPLE: when sap begins [present tense sounds clumsy here] to flow in maple trees;

SUN: when the sun's rays are warm in the spring;

THUNDER: when the spring thunder is heard, ushering in heavy rains that moisten the earth;

SEED PLANTING: when it is time to plant;

STRAWBERRY: when wild strawberries are ripe to eat;

BEAN: when the green beans are grown;

GREEN CORN: when the first corn is ripe;

HARVEST: when all the crops are harvested.

In addition to calendrics, the Mohawks performed curing rituals. Sick people frequently prescribed their own treatment based on their interpretations of their dreams. If they dreamed about a curing ceremony, they would request that the same rite be performed. Other types of curing rituals were conducted by members of "medicine societies." Each society had its own distinctive ceremonial cures. The choice of the society and the method of treatment were usually made by a specialist skilled in making diagnoses. This healer gave her or his opinion based on the patient's symptoms, dreams, or hidden messages observed in bowls of water or tea. Healers looked into the liquids and tried to see movement or signs coming from supernatural forces. Then members of the medicine society performed their rituals in the patient's house. Some cures included massaging the patient with ashes from hearths. Like the stirring of ashes at the start of Midwinter, this act, too, functioned as a metaphor for renewal.

In other cures, healers donned masks representing supernatural beings whose restorative powers were applied to a
patient. Masks had great spiritual meaning to the Mohawks.
Some masks, called false faces, were made of wood and were
associated with the spirits of the forest. Others, made of cornhusks, were linked to agricultural spirits. Masks were thought
to be alive. They were carved into a living tree and extracted
from the tree only when completed so that they retained the
tree's life forces. To keep their false faces alive, the Mohawks
periodically "fed" the masks tobacco.

Another major group of ceremonies was associated with
death. Funerals were held within a few days of a person's death
and were marked by condolence speeches given by members of
the moiety to which the deceased did not belong. Condolences
expressed sadness and sympathy for the bereaved relatives.
Societal balance and interdependence were symbolized by the
obligations each moiety fulfilled in conducting funerals for the
other group. The occasion of a person's death thus provided an
opportunity for a communal expression of unity.

For ten days after a death, food was set out for the
deceased's ghost, which was believed to remain nearby. Then,
to release the dead person's spirit, the Tenth-Day Feast was held.
During this rite, the personal possessions of the deceased were
distributed among the guests. People believed that only after
such a feast could a ghost begin its journey along the Milky
Way to the afterworld.

In addition to marking individual deaths, the Mohawks
conducted a ceremony once or twice a year to commemorate
everyone who had died since the last such rite. Special songs and
dances were performed to honor the dead and comfort the living.

Several themes were common to all Mohawk rituals. The
theme of renewal of life and health was expressed in Midwinter,
in seasonal calendrics, and in curing ceremonies. Thanksgivings
to the natural and supernatural worlds, which were recited at
the beginning and end of all ceremonies, demonstrated the

importance of mutual respect and reciprocity among all creatures and forces of the universe. Finally, death rites recognized bonds between the living and the dead.

In daily life, the Mohawks lived according to ethics of hospitality, generosity, and consideration for others. These principles were shown in the people's eagerness to share with others whatever foods or goods they possessed. They gave aid and comfort to each other in times of crisis, and they believed that people should live harmoniously and respect others' rights.

Unity was important in the political life of the Mohawks and their Iroquoian neighbors. Councils met periodically in each village and nation to discuss events of importance, plan communal activities, commemorate deaths of prominent people, and welcome visitors.

In the fourteenth or fifteenth century, the Mohawk Nation formed the Iroquois Confederacy with the Oneida, the Onondaga, the Cayuga, and the Seneca. Also known as the Five Nations and the Iroquois League, the confederacy's main purpose was to preserve peace among members. It was a complex organization designed to respect each nation's rights but also to make them responsible for reciprocal aid in times of trouble. The confederacy was symbolized by a great longhouse stretching from east to west across *Iroquois* territory. In the Mohawk language, it was called *Ganonsyonni* (ga-non-SHON-ni), meaning "the extended house," or *Rotinonsyonni* (ro-di-non-SHON-ni), meaning "They are of the extended house." In this longhouse, the Mohawks were the Keepers of the Eastern Door, for theirs was the easternmost Iroquois nation.

Confederacy chiefs were men chosen by elder women, or matrons, of their clan. Chiefs and matrons attained their positions because of personal skills, intelligence, good judgment, and generosity. A chief was installed for life during a ceremony in which he was crowned with a headdress of deer antlers. If a chief's conduct in councils or even his behavior in the community was deemed inappropriate, he could be deposed by the matrons of his clan. These women first warned the man about his unsatisfactory behavior. Then, if their warnings went unheeded, he was "dehorned"—impeached by removing his chiefly antler headdress.

According to Iroquois oral traditions, the confederacy was founded by two chiefs named Hiawatha (hi-ya-WA-ta) and Deganawida (de-ga-na-WEE-da). Hiawatha was of the Onondaga tribe, while Deganawida was born among the Huron Indians north of Lake Ontario. Both men, however, journeyed from their home to Mohawk territory and were later adopted by the Mohawks. After Hiawatha and Deganawida met in a Mohawk village, they began to discuss the idea of a *confederacy* that would unite all five nations in a great peace. Deganawida then traveled to the other nations to submit the plan for their consent. The first evening, he stayed at the house of a Mohawk woman and told her of his purpose, which she approved. This episode in the story symbolized the necessity of gaining women's consent to actions taken by the league.

All of the Iroquois chiefs accepted the plan proposed by Deganawida and Hiawatha, except for the belligerent Onondaga leader Tadodaho (ta-do-DA-ho). Tadodaho at last agreed to join after it was promised that he would be "first among equals." To show respect for Tadodaho and for Onondaga territory as the geographic center of Iroquois lands, league councils were always held in the principal Onondaga village. The Onondaga are therefore known as the "fire keepers." They had the honor of announcing council meetings.

Chiefs held confederacy meetings at least once a year, but they could meet whenever an important issue needed to be discussed. Councils were concerned with intertribal matters, trade negotiations with foreigners, and deliberations of war and peace.

There were originally fifty confederacy chiefs, each with a name or title that was passed on to another man of his clan after his death or demotion. However, two of the titles, those of the league's founders—Deganawida (also known as the Peace-maker) and Hiawatha—were always left unfilled. Each nation had its own titles: the Onondaga had fourteen titles, the Cayuga had ten, the Mohawk and the Oneida each had nine, and the Seneca had eight.

The Five Nations were divided into two moieties, paralleling the kinship division of clans. One moiety—the Elders—consisted of the Mohawk, the Onondaga, and the Seneca. The Oneida and the Cayuga constituted the other, or the Younger, moiety. Seating at council meetings was arranged by nation and moiety. The Mohawk and the Seneca sat on one side, the Oneida and the Cayuga sat on the other, and the Onondaga took the central position before the council fire.

All decisions of the confederacy had to be unanimous. In reaching a consensus, deliberations proceeded according to a fixed sequence of events. The topic of discussion was announced by the Onondagas, who then "gave" it to the Mohawks for their consideration. When they reached a decision, they passed the topic to the Seneca chiefs. After reaching their conclusions, the Senecas passed it back to the Mohawks, who announced their joint decision and relayed the topic "across the fire" to the other moiety. The Oneidas and the Cayugas deliberated next, passing the matter between them. After the Oneidas declared their decision to the Mohawks, a Mohawk chief announced the results to the Onondagas. If the Onondagas agreed, the decision was unanimous, and the matter was settled with a final ceremonial declaration by Tadodaho. At the conclusion of a session, the actions of the council were "read into" the belts of wampum that recorded significant events. Woven patterns or images in the belts were mnemonic devices that helped people recall important agreements or historical episodes.

If a consensus was not achieved at a council meeting, the problem could be given back to the Mohawks for further deliberation, starting the process of negotiation once more.

Wampum belts like this one were often used as part of the Mohawks' attire to commemorate important events. Clam shells, which were obtained through trade with Indians on Long Island and coastal New Jersey, were cut into pieces and made into small beads that were strung together to make these belts.

If unanimity was impossible to reach, the matter was set aside, and the council fire was covered up with ashes. This ritual act marked the inability of the league chiefs to "roll their words into one bundle." It was so important that all be of One Heart, One Mind, One Law that the league could take no action without unanimous agreement.

In addition to civil or peace chiefs, war chiefs from each nation had responsibility for discussing and planning military expeditions. These men could have their opinions heard through selected speakers at confederacy meetings, but they did not participate in decision-making. Clan matrons or other prominent women could similarly appoint speakers to voice their opinions to the league chiefs.

This complex political structure achieved remarkable results over the course of several centuries. By the beginning of the seventeenth century, the Mohawk and the other Iroquois nations wielded considerable power in the Northeast, extending their influence far beyond their own territory. Skillful Iroquois diplomats negotiated agreements with other nations, backed by the success of their warriors. And the league itself rested on a secure cultural foundation, sustained by the social and economic contributions of Iroquois women and men.

3

Keepers of the Eastern Door

The beginning of the eighteenth century was a pivotal period for American Indians. By this time, only a limited number of Europeans had landed on the shores of North America. They came as traders, explorers, *missionaries*, and settlers. At first, Indians welcomed these newcomers—mostly because they wanted European trade goods. However, early immigrants from Europe were to bring much more to the Indians. In time, their arrival would prove to be the start of an overwhelming tide of change.

The Mohawks had received news of Europeans long before they met white men face-to-face. From other Indians they heard about new types of tools, utensils, clothing, and weapons that Europeans offered in exchange for beaver furs. Europeans desired these furs in almost endless numbers because beaver hats and collars were the rage of fashion in seventeenth-century Holland, France, and England.

A fanciful drawing by a seventeenth-century French artist of a tattooed Mohawk man. The turtle on his thigh probably represents his clan.

Involvement in this trade had both positive and negative effects on Indian cultures. On the positive side, it allowed the Indians to improve their living conditions in several ways. For the first time, they obtained goods made of metal, such as iron kettles, knives, scissors, nails, axes, and sword blades. They also used iron hinges to fasten shelves in their longhouses. Metal objects were more durable than the earthen pottery and stone or bone implements that Native people had previously made and used. Woolen cloth from European factories was also greatly desired by Indians. The Mohawks especially liked the heavy duffel cloth sold at Dutch trading posts because it provided better protection against the frequent rains than did the beaver skins that people had traditionally worn. Although duffel cloth came in several colors, the Mohawks preferred subdued shades of blue or gray because these did not startle and frighten away animals in the forest.

The Mohawks so favored the tools and utensils brought by Europeans that they soon stopped learning traditional skills such as pottery making and toolmaking. The goods that at first had been considered novelties and luxuries rapidly became necessities of life. The Mohawks' growing dependence on European goods forced them to alter their economy. In order to obtain trade items, men had to trap beaver in increasing numbers. Before European contact, the Mohawks had been careful to hunt only as many animals as they needed for food and clothing. Enough animals therefore survived and reproduced to ensure an adequate supply the next year. With growing desires for trade goods, however, people abandoned their efforts to conserve the animal population and instead began to trap many more animals than they had in the past.

In a very short time, all the beaver in the lands controlled by the Mohawks were gone. The situation was desperate; without beaver pelts people could not obtain the goods they now needed to perform their daily activities. Louis de Lahontan, a French traveler of the time, commented on the Mohawks' plight in his journal. He concluded that without beaver skins they "would be starved to death, or at least obliged to leave their country."

The Mohawks had two alternatives. One was to withdraw from trade. Such a choice was obviously unacceptable because it would have meant giving up those items that had improved their lives. The second alternative was to try to obtain pelts from those

Indian groups that still had an abundance of beavers in their territory. Since these peoples also wanted to trade animal skins to Europeans, the Mohawks were compelled to obtain the skins by force. And so began decades of intense intertribal warfare.

One of the first major conflicts occurred in the summer of 1609, when a group of Mohawk warriors were attacked by a contingent of Huron Indians, Algonkian Indians, and French soldiers led by French explorer Samuel de Champlain. The Hurons and the Algonkians were already enemies of the Mohawks. The two groups had previously entered into alliances with France and sought French aid in a campaign against the Mohawks.

The Indian and French allies set out against a Mohawk force that was rumored to be near a large lake in present-day northeastern New York, later known as Lake Champlain. The two groups of warriors met on July 29, 1609. Champlain's force, made up of approximately sixty men, was greatly outnumbered by the two hundred Mohawk fighters who were led by three chiefs. According to Indian custom, the enemies approached each other and began shooting their arrows. Champlain and his men, however, surprised the Mohawks with something they had never seen before—muskets. Champlain opened fire on the Mohawk chiefs, killing two of them immediately. The third chief was wounded and died soon afterward.

The Mohawks were terrified by the sound of guns and by the instantaneous death they caused. As Champlain's men continued to shoot, the Indians fled for their lives. Champlain was satisfied with the success of this battle because he mistakenly believed that it proved French superiority and confirmed that his force's victory over the Mohawks was inevitable.

The following year, Mohawk warriors fought against another group of Algonkians and French troops at a place near the Richelieu River in present-day Quebec. Again French soldiers used muskets, killing as many as one hundred Mohawk men. And again the Indians fled in fear of the

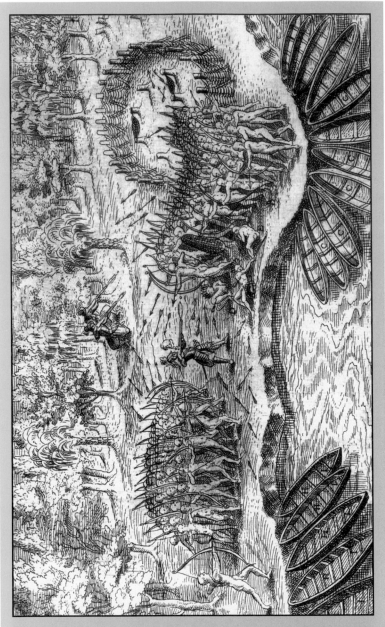

This engraving depicts the 1609 battle between the Mohawks and a group of French soldiers and Huron and Algonkian Indians, led by explorer Samuel de Champlain. The engagement was pitched near present-day Lake Champlain and was significant in that it was the first time Mohawks had faced muskets in battle.

guns' deadly effect. Although the Mohawks were alarmed at the outcome of these battles, they were not easily dislodged from their lands or dissuaded from trying to tighten their control over trade.

At this time, more and more French were gathering along the St. Lawrence River in the north. Meanwhile, Dutch traders were establishing posts near the Hudson River in present-day New York. The principal Dutch post, opened in 1615, was called Fort Orange. (The fort would be renamed Albany by the English in 1664.) It was located near the territories of both the Mohawk and the Mahican Indians. War broke out almost immediately between these two Indian peoples for control over access to the fort. Both groups wanted to stop other Indians from trading directly with Dutch merchants. They each hoped to increase their own power by forcing others to trade through them as go-betweens. After the wars ended in 1619 with Mohawk victories, the Mohawks replaced the Mahicans as the main suppliers of beaver pelts to Dutch dealers. Meanwhile, the Iroquois Confederacy had signed a commercial *treaty* with the Dutch in 1618. Although the agreement concerned all five Iroquois Nations, the Mohawks figured prominently in dealings with Dutch traders because their territory was closest to Fort Orange.

Dutch suppliers introduced the Mohawks to a wide range of foreign products. Metalware, such as brass kettles and iron hunting tools, was especially desired. In addition, the Mohawks obtained duffel cloth, biscuits, and flour. They also traded with the Dutch for wampum, which was of great ceremonial value to the Iroquois. Wampum was produced by the Montauk, Shinnecock, and other Indian nations living on what is now Long Island, New York; then a territory colonized by Dutch merchants and settlers. The Dutch contracted with Long Island Indians to increase their production of wampum because it was in such high demand by the Iroquois. (For additional information on the importance of wampum, enter "wampum beads" into any search engine and browse the many sites listed.)

Warfare between the Mohawk and the Mahican tribes erupted again in the mid-1620s, ending in 1628 with another Mohawk victory. During this period, tensions in the area had increased due to encroachments of Dutch settlers on Indian lands around Fort Orange. As colonists arrived in greater numbers, Indians and Europeans began to compete more than ever for farmland and hunting areas. At the same time, the beaver population in eastern and central New York continued to decline because of heavy hunting, which in turn increased intertribal competition.

A Mohawk leader expressed his nation's dilemma in a conversation with Dutch officials in 1659: "The Dutch say we are brothers, and joined together with chains, but that lasts only as long as we have beavers; after that no attention is paid to us."

The "attention" that the Mohawks wanted was access to European products, and they were prepared to secure trade by engaging in warfare against their neighbors. Intense conflicts raged in the region from the 1630s through the 1650s. Mohawk raids during this period included attacks against the Pequot and the Narragansett Nation in New England, the Huron in southern Ontario, the Montagnais near Tadoussac in northeastern Quebec, the Abenaki and Maliseet in the Canadian Maritime Provinces, the Ottawa and Algonquins in the Ottawa River valley, and the Neutral and Erie in the Great Lakes region. In all these areas, the Mohawks and their Iroquois allies were victorious. They compelled other Native peoples to supply them with furs and to deal with European traders through them. One tactic the Mohawks used was to set up ambushes along the Hudson and St. Lawrence Rivers, attacking travelers who carried animal skins en route to the trading posts at Fort Orange, Montreal, or Quebec. The Mohawks were so successful that they were able to take as much as one-quarter of the furs transported along the rivers. As a result, some groups, such as the Huron, Neutral, and Erie, were forced to flee from their ancestral lands, most of them eventually relocating farther west. Mohawk prowess was enhanced when Dutch traders began selling guns to them in the 1640s, giving the Mohawks an advantage unavailable to other Indians at that time.

In addition to the turmoil created by armed conflict, the mid-seventeenth century witnessed incalculable Indian deaths from the ravages of European diseases. When Europeans arrived in North America, they unwittingly brought with them germs that caused epidemics of deadly diseases such as smallpox and measles. Because these viruses were not native to North America, Indian populations had never developed immunities to them. Therefore, when the germs were introduced to the Indians through contact with Europeans, the organisms' deadly force was impossible to withstand. Within a few decades, thousands of Indians in the Northeast had died. Families and sometimes entire villages were decimated by a single epidemic.

During this time, the Mohawks increased their involvement with Europeans. Commercial dealings with Dutch traders were expanded after Mohawk victories over other Indian groups. The Mohawks now also traded with English merchants, who were enlarging their sphere of influence and attempting to wrest control over commerce from the Dutch. In addition, the *tribe* periodically established contacts with French merchants in Montreal and Quebec.

By 1640, only about one thousand Dutch had settled in the entire colony of New Netherland and perhaps one hundred in the vicinity of Fort Orange. But within a few years, settlement increased rapidly. Because the soil in Mohawk territory was rich and productive, it was treasured by Dutch farmers for the planting of crops and orchards. The Dutch government then adopted an official policy of purchasing land fairly from the Indians. They were vitally interested in establishing and maintaining good trade relations with Indian groups and did not want to anger them by allowing unscrupulous land dealings. But despite official intentions, Dutch settlers tried to occupy Indian land without legally purchasing it. In the 1650s, the

Dutch set up local courts for administering their colonies and heard many complaints brought by Mohawk people against illegal expansion of Dutch farms into their territory.

English settlers also made inroads into eastern and central New York from the areas they colonized in New England. In 1664, the English took control of lands claimed by the Dutch as well, owing to English victories in conflicts with Holland fought both in North America and in Europe. In the same year, Mohawk and Seneca representatives concluded a commercial agreement with English merchants, pledging to shift their allegiance to the English.

However, new hostilities were soon created by the movement of English settlers into Mohawk territory. England at first allowed settlers to negotiate land deals with the Indians without official supervision. The settlers did not always deal fairly with the Natives, and the resulting tensions increased as more English immigrants arrived. In some cases, Mohawk individuals sought English aid by turning their land over to the jurisdiction of the Crown. The English government then assumed legal responsibility for safeguarding Mohawk land rights. But this maneuver did not solve the problem, because local officials sometimes disobeyed policies set down in London.

In the early 1690s, colonial governors tried to encourage more settlement by granting lands within Mohawk territory to English citizens. Then, in 1696, the English appointed a commissioner to record colonial land transactions, including those between Indians and settlers. The following year, two Mohawks brought a serious complaint to the commissioner, declaring that they had been tricked into signing a deed granting an Englishman control over some of their land. The fraudulent deed covered an enormous area, extending for fifty miles on both sides of the Mohawk River west of Albany. According to the Indians' testimony, Godfrey Dellius, a minister living in their community, had advised them that they should appoint him as their guardian to protect their land. The two Mohawks

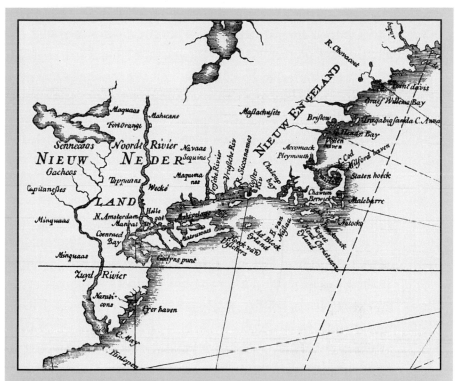

A 1630 map of New Netherland. The main trading post between the Dutch and Mohawks was at Fort Orange (seen here), which later became Albany. The Mohawks defeated the neighboring Mahicans in 1619 for trading rights to the fort.

stated that they then signed a document they thought was the agreement of guardianship but turned out to be a deed of sale. The Indians' claim was recognized as just, and the land deal was annulled.

Perhaps because of the huge amount of land involved, injustice in this incident was brought to light. But most likely many other fraudulent deals went undetected and unredressed. Thousands of acres of Mohawk land were undoubtedly stolen by similar means. Colonial administrators often helped in this process. Many members of local assemblies were themselves wealthy landowners. They were in a position to establish policies and make decisions from which they could benefit financially at the expense of Indian peoples.

Despite these serious problems, the Mohawks remained loyal to their English allies. They continued to trade with the English and aid them in battles against the enemies of England, most notably France. But even though the Mohawks were the enemies of the French in military matters, the Indians wanted to establish commercial relations with them. In 1653, representatives of the two groups signed a treaty guaranteeing the peaceful exchange of valuables. Still, the Mohawks preferred trading with the English because their goods were of superior quality to those of the French and could be obtained at a lower cost. In fact, one of the Mohawks' motives in signing treaties with the French was to put pressure on English merchants to keep their prices low. The Mohawks reasoned that if the two European nations had to compete with each other for Indian trade, neither one could exert monopoly control. By negotiating agreements with both powers, the Mohawks demonstrated their skill at developing strategies by which they would prosper economically.

The arrival of French missionaries also increased contact between the Mohawks and the French traders. In the early 1600s, missionaries from France began to contact Indians in the Northeast. *Jesuit* priests first took up missionary work in 1610, visiting Algonkian and Huron allies of the French. The Mohawks did not encounter missionaries until 1642. In that year, a Catholic priest named Isaac Jogues made a journey to their territory in hopes of establishing a *mission* there but the trip was not successful. When Jogues departed from the region, he carelessly left behind a black box, which he had probably used as a storage container.

During the next four years, waves of disease struck the Mohawk communities Jogues had visited. Crops also failed. Because the Mohawks believed that disease could be caused by witchcraft, they attributed their illnesses to the black box. In the words of another French priest, Father Gabriel Lalemant, the Mohawks came to the following conclusion: "Sickness having fallen upon their bodies after [Jogues's] departure, and worms having perhaps damaged their corn, these poor blind creatures have believed that the Father had left them the Demon among them, and that all our discourses aimed only to exterminate them."

Although Jogues did not knowingly cause harm to the Mohawks, he may actually have been a carrier of the deadly smallpox virus that spread rapidly among their villagers. Believing the priest was responsible for the disasters that struck them, the Mohawks executed Jogues when he returned to their village in 1646. Members of the Wolf and Turtle clans opposed the execution, but it was carried out by Bear clan leaders nonetheless. And although Jogues' death caused renewed friction between the Mohawks and French, Father Lalemant observed: "It is true that, speaking humanly, these Barbarians have apparent reasons for reproaching us—inasmuch as the scourges which humble the proud precede us or accompany us wherever we go."

Despite setbacks, Jesuit missionaries returned to Mohawk territory in 1656 and 1657. At that time, the Mohawks actively encouraged these visits. In fact, when priests proposed journeys to the Iroquois nations, both the Mohawk and Onondaga suggested that they build the first French mission among the Iroquois in their territory. These nations recognized that friendship with the Jesuits would be well regarded by French officials and could strengthen commercial agreements. At an official meeting between the Iroquois and the missionaries in Quebec, the Onondagas claimed that the priests should come to them because they had been the first to start negotiations about the missions. When it was the Mohawks' turn to speak, they invoked the symbolic metaphor of the confederacy as a longhouse and of the Mohawks as Keepers of the Eastern Door. A Mohawk orator, quoted by Father Joseph LeMerciér, declared: "Ought not one to enter a house by the door, and not by the chimney or roof of the cabin, unless he be a thief, and wish to take the inmates by surprise? We, the Five Iroquois Nations, compose but one cabin; we maintain but one fire; and we have, from time immemorial, dwelt under the same roof. Well, then, will you not enter the cabin by the door? It is with us Anniehronnons [Mohawks], that you should begin; whereas you, by beginning with the Onnontaehronnon [Onondagas], try to enter by the roof and through the chimney." Despite the eloquence of this argument, the Jesuits established missions among the Onondagas. But later, in 1656, they traveled to Mohawk territory.

On the whole, missionary efforts to convert the Mohawks met with very limited success. Only a few Natives listened seriously to the priests' sermons. The Mohawks' motives in welcoming the priests had been more economic than religious. They had wanted to establish themselves as intermediaries in French commerce and hoped to compel members of the other four Iroquois nations to trade through them. Intertribal competition therefore occasionally spread within the Iroquois Confederacy as well as between the Iroquois and other Indian groups.

Nevertheless, missionaries offered advice to French officials about how best to maintain friendships with the Mohawks. Even though the Mohawks lacked enthusiasm for religious conversion, the priests' statements about the Indians and their culture were favorable while peace lasted. Father Simon Le Moyne, who visited Mohawk villages in 1656 and 1657, commented: "No hospitals are needed among them, because there are neither mendicants nor paupers as long as there are any rich people among them. Their kindness, humanity, and courtesy not only make them liberal with what they have, but cause them to possess hardly anything except in common. A whole village must be without corn before any individual can be obliged to endure privation."

When the fragile peace turned to war, as often happened, the Jesuits' remarks also turned bitter. They counseled the government to step up attacks against the Mohawks. They advised that if the Mohawks could be defeated, the other four Iroquois nations would abandon war and agree to treaties with France. The Mohawks, however, remained unbeaten, and the Jesuits were compelled to write with respect, if not approval, of Mohawk military skills. In 1660, Father Lalemant offered the following review:

> The Agnieronnons [Mohawks] have had to fight with all their neighbors—with the Abnaquois [Abenakis], who are eastward of them; on the south with the Andastogehronnons [Andastes], a people inhabiting the shores of Virginia; with the Hurons on the west; and with all the Algonkian nations scattered throughout the north. But what is more astonishing is that they actually hold dominion over 500 leagues around, although their numbers are small; for the Agnieronnons do not exceed 500 men able to bear arms, who occupy three or four villages.

During a period of intensifying warfare in the 1660s, French forces organized a strike against Mohawk villages. An army of twelve hundred French troops and six hundred Indian allies under the leadership of Marquis Prouville de Tracy entered Mohawk territory. Advance word arrived in time to warn villagers, who fled to the forests for safety. French soldiers then burned the empty houses and surrounding cornfields.

A further complication in relations between the Mohawks and Europeans was set in motion in 1667 when Jesuits persuaded several Mohawk converts to leave their ancestral lands and resettle in missions near Montreal. The priests argued that because the converts were distrusted by their relatives and neighbors, they might become targets of retaliation as warfare intensified. The missionaries further claimed that Christian Mohawks would be safe only near French forts. After listening to these arguments, a group of Catholic Mohawks established a new village on the south side of the St. Lawrence River at La Prairie. Attracting Mohawk and

Oneida Indians, the settlement's population grew throughout the 1670s. In 1676, it was moved upriver to Sault St. Louis (present-day Lachine Rapids) because the soil at La Prairie was too damp for growing corn. The village was renamed Kahnawake (gah-na-WA-ge), meaning "at the rapids." The appellation had symbolic significance for these people because it had previously been the name of a Mohawk village in what is now New York State.

Mohawks remaining in New York were alarmed by the departure of the Christians for several reasons. First, it was a sign of a deep rift in Mohawk unity. Because the Mohawks valued the principle of One Heart, One Mind, One Law, such a split was especially disturbing. Second, many Mohawks worried that the French would exercise political as well as religious influence over the converts. They feared that the French would persuade the Christian Indians to fight against their kin. This worry was well founded. Kahnawake Mohawks initially pledged neutrality in Iroquois-French conflicts, but they were often drawn into battles on the side of France. They also traveled as ambassadors to the Mohawks in New York, where they tried, without success, to convince their kin to stop fighting the French and instead take up arms against English forces.

During this period, another mission for Mohawk Indians was established by an order of French Sulpician priests. In 1676, they founded the village of Kanesatake (ga-ne-sa-DA-ge) on the island of Montreal. The settlement was soon relocated to land a short distance west of Montreal along the Ottawa River, where it has remained since. The new site was favored by French authorities because it gave them a friendly post on the Ottawa River leading to the Great Lakes. Converts at Kanesatake were from various Iroquoian and Algonkian groups, but the majority were Mohawks. They, too, sometimes fought against their former neighbors.

At both Kahnawake and Kanesatake, people attempted to continue with their traditional way of life as much as possible.

They succeeded in maintaining their economies and clan systems. However, they abandoned several customs that were criticized by Jesuit teachings. Jesuits stressed the importance of marital bonds and therefore condemned the Mohawk custom of allowing couples to divorce easily. They also opposed the Indians' tendency to indulge their children. Instead, they preached that children must be obedient and should be punished if they misbehaved. Finally, the priests tried to eradicate Mohawk beliefs about the importance of interpreting and fulfilling one's dreams. To Jesuit thinking, these practices were signs of devil worship. Over the next few decades, converts were influenced by the missionaries' teachings and gradually adopted European values. These changes, of course, made converts appear strange to the Mohawks remaining in New York and gave further evidence of French treachery.

Meanwhile, despite the alliance between the Mohawks and the English, conflicts increased as the number of English settlers grew and as their appetite for land seemed to become insatiable. In the early years of contact, Indians had far outnumbered the newcomers. But in a relatively short time, the balance shifted because of the extraordinarily high rate of Indian deaths from disease and the huge number of immigrants from Europe. When the English first arrived in North America, they needed the help of Indians for their survival. But as early as 1684, less than eighty years after the first permanent English settlement was established in North America, an Iroquois chief made the following remark to Colonel Thomas Dongan, an English official in Albany: "You are a mighty sachem [leader] and we but a small people. When the English first came to New York, Virginia and Maryland, they were but a small people and we a large nation, and we finding they were good people gave them land and dealt civilly by them; Now that you are grown numerous and we decreased, you must protect us from the French."

Even though the Mohawks remained allied to the English, they distrusted English motives and feared that their lands would be taken by colonists. The Indians also were uneasy about the lack of full English support in campaigns against French forces. Needing to protect their own safety, the Mohawks negotiated several peace treaties with the French. Although these treaties were soon dissolved by actions on both sides, English officials were threatened by any sign of Mohawk friendship with France. At a meeting in 1691 between the Mohawks and Colonel Henry Sloughter, governor of New York, the Englishman reproached the Indians by saying: "You must keep the Enemy in perpetual alarm." To this, a Mohawk leader responded, "Why don't you say, 'We will keep the Enemy in perpetual alarm.'"

In the same year, the Mohawks were given proof of the validity of their complaints. A force of English and Iroquois warriors attacked French forts in Montreal in August 1691. But because the English had not sent enough troops to counteract French forces, the campaign was unsuccessful, and the Mohawks lost a large number of men.

At a meeting held in 1692 with Governor Richard Ingoldsby, who replaced Sloughter after the colonel's death, the Mohawks repeated their misgivings about English intentions. Their speeches told of their predicament:

> We are all subjects of one great King and Queen, we have one head, one heart, one interest, and are all engaged in the same war. We are resolved to carry on the war, though we know we only are in danger of being losers. Pray do you prosecute the war with the same resolution. You are strong and have many people. You have a great king who is able to hold out long. We are but a small people, declining daily, by the men we lose in this war, we do our utmost to destroy the enemy; but how strange does it seem to us! How unaccountable! That while our great king is so inveterate against the French, and you so earnest with us to carry on the war, that powder is now sold dearer to us than ever? We are poor, and not able

to buy while we neglect hunting; and we cannot hunt and carry on the war at the same time. You desire us to keep the Enemy in perpetual alarm; Is it not to secure your own frontiers? Why then not one word of your people that are to join us? How comes it that none of our Brethren fastened in the same chain with us, offer their helping hand in this general war? Pray make plain to us this mystery? How can they and we be subjects of the same great king, and not be engaged in the same war?

The same year, six hundred French troops under Count Louis de Frontenac attacked several Mohawk villages. One of Frontenac's motives was to show the Mohawks that they could not depend on the English for protection. He was correct. French soldiers were able to destroy three villages and capture three hundred prisoners, including one hundred warriors and two hundred noncombatant men, women, and children.

By the end of the seventeenth century, turmoil in the Northeast continued unabated. The Mohawks and their Iroquois allies renewed attacks against several Indian peoples. They ranged as far west as Lake Superior in raids against the Huron, Neutral, and Petun tribes, who had relocated there. They made expeditions to the south as well, reaching to Virginia and the Carolinas.

The turn of the eighteenth century also witnessed increasing expansion of English colonies, which encroached ever more on Mohawk territory. Skilled strategists among the Mohawks attempted to strike a balance with the English and French so that they could remain independent of both colonial powers. Although they were successful for a time, stability for the Mohawks was to be short-lived.

4

Deepening
Crises

At the beginning of the eighteenth century, the Mohawks retained their dominance over Indian groups in the Northeast. Many of their enemies had been defeated, forced to abandon their territories, and resettle farther west. Others remained in the East but pledged not to take up arms against the Iroquois. Some were compelled to pay symbolic tribute in wampum to the Mohawks who represented the victorious confederacy. The league itself remained strong. The Iroquois were well respected by European powers as much for their skillful diplomacy as for their military success. In 1720, Pierre Charlevoix, a French Recollet priest, observed:

> As the Iroquois were situated between us [French] and the English, they soon found that both would be under the necessity of keeping well with them; and indeed it has been the chief care of both colonies, to gain them over to their own party, or, at least, to

persuade them to stand neutral: and as they were persuaded that if either of these nations should entirely get the ascendant over the other, they must soon be subjected themselves; they have found the secret of balancing their success; and if we reflect that their whole force united has never exceeded five or six thousand combatants, and that it is a great while since they have diminished more than one half, we must needs allow, they must have used infinite abilities and address.

But the previous one hundred years had taken a heavy toll on the Mohawk Nation. Many Mohawks had been killed, both from deadly European diseases and from the scourge of warfare that continued without respite. The land of the People of the Place of Flint was diminished in size as the Dutch and English colonies expanded. Because of these difficult conditions, many Mohawk Indians left their traditional lands, migrating northward to the protected missions at Kahnawake and Kanesatake near Montreal.

In the second year of the eighteenth century, the Iroquois Confederacy signed a peace treaty with French representatives in Quebec. However, like all the others before it, the treaty was soon broken. Hostilities in Europe led to war in North America. In 1702, Queen Anne's War erupted between England and France. As in past conflicts, this war engulfed the Indians, who were pressured into aiding their respective allies. During the war, which lasted until 1713, the Iroquois fought on the side of the English. France had the help of several Algonkian peoples. The majority of the Mohawks were loyal to the English, but French leaders in Quebec persuaded the Catholic Mohawks at Kahnawake and Kanesatake to aid their cause. Deep divisions within the Mohawk Nation grew when relatives and former neighbors fought on different sides.

As Queen Anne's War continued, the English government wanted to strengthen its alliance with the Iroquois. In an attempt to win favor, Protestant missionaries from England began working in Indian communities in the early eighteenth century. The English saw that the Catholic Mohawks had shifted their allegiance from England to France, so they hoped that good relations between the English ministers and the Mohawk communities would increase the Indians' support for England. Several missions were established but none attracted any strong interest from the Mohawks in that period.

In another attempt to encourage goodwill, the British sponsored a trip to England in 1710 by the so-called Four Indian Kings. Three of these "kings" were prominent Mohawk leaders, including a chief known as Hendrick, or Tee yee Neen Ho Ga Row, who became an important ally in later British wars. The kings were entertained in London, where they met with British officials and had an audience with Queen Anne. At the meeting, Indian leaders asked the queen for protection from French attacks. She responded by ordering the construction of a new fort and chapel, called Fort Hunter, along the Mohawk River. (For additional information on this Mohawk leader, enter "Mohawk Chief Hendrick" into any search engine and browse the many sites listed.)

Although Fort Hunter provided security against French raids, it did nothing to stop encroachment on Mohawk land by British colonists. In fact, the presence of Fort Hunter encouraged settlement by Europeans because, living near the fort, they felt protected. In the previous century, the western-most colonial communities had been located near Schenectady, but by 1720, larger numbers of settlers had moved farther west. During the next decade, many German immigrants also invaded the Mohawk and Hudson River valleys. This new wave of immigration encroached on Native communities. The city of Albany itself laid fraudulent claim to nearby Mohawk territory. Fearing that all their land would be occupied by settlers, the Mohawks in 1733 turned over a large tract of land—including twelve hundred acres of meadow and two thousand acres of

Chief Hendrick, or Tee Yee Neen Ho Ga Row, was one of four Mohawk kings who traveled to London and met with England's Queen Anne in 1710. Though a supporter of the British, Hendrick did not shy away from speaking up against the colonists' encroachment on Indian land. As a result, the British undertook a policy of looking into all land deals and protecting Indian rights.

forest—to the English king, George II. The agreement between the Mohawks and the king stipulated that neither could sell nor transfer any of the land without the consent of the other.

The Mohawks hoped that their lands were finally safe from settlers' advances. However, the British government was either unable or unwilling to protect Natives from illegal sales. Throughout the 1730s and 1740s, the Mohawks brought numerous complaints to local officials, asserting that colonists were moving into their territory. After a careful review of deeds, a British surveyor general, Cadwallader Colden, found that many of the documents transferred ownership of larger tracts of land than the Mohawk sellers had intended. Because the Indians were unfamiliar with European methods of measuring land and could not read the deeds, they were easily cheated out of hundreds and even thousands of acres. Colden recommended that Mohawk lands be properly measured and surveyed with Indians present in order to protect their rights.

During this period, the confederacy was enlarged by the addition of a sixth nation, the Tuscarora. The Tuscaroras were Iroquoian peoples, closely related linguistically and culturally to the five original league members. At the time of European contact, they lived in present-day Virginia. Later, when English settlements there expanded into Indian territories, the Tuscaroras sought refuge in the north. They asked the powerful Iroquois for protection and were admitted to the confederacy in 1722.

In the following decades, British missionaries renewed attempts to convert the Mohawks. They rebuilt the chapel at Fort Hunter and opened schools at two Mohawk villages. By 1750, many of the Mohawks in New York were nominally Christian. Along with religious teachings, missionaries encouraged the Indians to trust and support the British. Still, complaints continued about settlers' encroachments upon Mohawk land. In 1753, at a meeting that took place in Albany between Mohawk leaders and Governor Clinton, the Mohawk chief Hendrick spoke bitterly of the colonists' occupation of Indian land. He carefully detailed case after case of illegalities:

> Barclay, Pitchetts wife. We let her have a little spot of land and she takes in more and more every year.
>
> We have a complaint against Arent Stevens. He bought a tract of land of us, and when the surveyor came to survey it, we showed him how far to go, and then Arent Stevens came and told him he had employed him and made him go a great deal further.
>
> We have another complaint against Conradt Gunterman. We gave him a tract of land out of charity but he takes in more which we have not given or sold him.
>
> Johannes Lawyers Patent at Stonerabie to no further than the Creek. He has taken up six miles further than the Creek.
>
> Honnes Clock claims an island below the Indian Castle at Conojohary which was never sold to any person.

Although Clinton tried to reassure Hendrick that Mohawk accusations would be properly investigated, Hendrick replied that the "covenant chain of friendship" between his nation and Great Britain was broken. Alarmed by the possibility of losing Iroquois allegiance, the government in London ordered a full accounting of land deals and protection of Indian rights. However, as in the past, colonial administrators were ineffective. They rarely came to the aid of the Indians; instead, they turned a blind eye to settlers' abuses.

One particularly serious complaint involved a huge tract of eight hundred thousand acres of land north of the Mohawk River and west of the Hudson River. The attorney general of New York, Sampson Broughton, said that he had purchased this land from the Mohawk Nation in 1703 for £60 (about $150). The Indians asserted that Broughton's claim was false. They declared that the area he claimed was too large, that no money had ever been paid, and that the transaction was invalid in any case because only two of the three Mohawk

clans had agreed to the sale. Although the Mohawks repeat-
edly sought redress in this case, it was not until 1768 that
the government completed an investigation. An agreement
was finally reached in which the Mohawks consented to sell
the eastern portion of the original tract for $5,000. They
retained a smaller section to the west.

As more settlers moved into the Mohawk Valley, trading
posts expanded their operations, relying on both Native and
immigrant commerce. Posts were built all along the Mohawk
River and even farther west as an increased British military
presence made colonists and merchants feel secure. Although
many Mohawks prospered from trade, their anger over
unscrupulous land transactions made them wary of long-term
British intentions.

Despite their misgivings, the Mohawks fulfilled pledges of
aid for Great Britain's cause during the French and Indian War
(1754–1763). This conflict would be the final major battle
between England and France for control of what is now the
eastern United States. Many Mohawk warriors fought and died
helping the British. Hendrick Peters, or Theyanoguin, was
among the casualties, dying at the Battle of Lake George in 1755.
The war ended with a British victory. In the peace agreement
between the two European adversaries, Indian rights to their
lands were recognized. In spite of British pledges, the forty thousand acres originally granted to the Mohawks at Kahnawake
near Montreal were immediately reduced by half.

After the end of the war, France was forced to withdraw
its armies from the Northeast, which left the Iroquois looking
forward to a lasting peace. But even though the Mohawks had
fought as loyal allies of Great Britain, they did not receive
the rewards of victory. As settlers arrived in ever-increasing
numbers and occupied Indian territory, the Mohawks tried to
keep what little land they had left.

At this time, the English government also began doubting
its own security in North America. Colonial rebelliousness

alarmed English officials. They realized that if the Iroquois were not satisfied with British protection, the Indians might turn against the Crown as well. Britain was therefore forced to listen to Iroquois complaints. They negotiated a treaty at Fort Stanwix in 1768 that established definite boundaries between Indian and British territory.

Some colonial officials also recognized the injustices that had been committed against the Indians and seriously attempted to make amends. Among these was Sir William Johnson, who had formerly traded with the Mohawks and had served as a superintendent of Indian affairs for New York. He often spoke on the Mohawks' behalf, intervening in conflicts between Indians and settlers. However, the gap between individual intentions and government actions was as wide as ever.

By the 1770s, many colonists were indeed rebelling against British authority. The rebels recognized the role that the Iroquois could play in helping or hindering their cause. In 1775, Iroquois leaders were invited to Albany for a meeting with the rebels—or Americans—led by Philip Schuyler. At that time, the Americans believed that the best they could hope for was Iroquoian neutrality. The Mohawks at the meeting raised issues of land claims against colonists. After the rebels gave words of assurance, the Iroquois pledged to be neutral if the colonists did indeed revolt. In return, the Americans promised to give the Indians a store of supplies, especially warm clothing.

The Continental Congress—the legislature established in 1774 to express colonial grievances against British policy—also tried to secure the friendship of Iroquois leaders. In the summer of 1775, the Continental Congress sent a message to the confederacy: "In our consultation we have judged it proper and necessary to send you this talk, as we are upon the same island, that you may be informed of the reasons of this great Council. . . . This is a family quarrel between us and old England. We desire you to remain at home, and not join on either side, but keep the hatchet buried deep."

For their part, the British attempted to use their long-standing alliance with the Iroquois to convince the Indians to fight against the revolutionaries. In July 1775, Sir Frederick Haldimand, governor of Canada, met with Mohawk leaders and told them: "Now is the time for you to help the King. The war has begun. Assist the King now, and you will find it to your advantage. Go now and fight for your possessions, and whatever you lose of your property during the war, the King will make up to you when peace returns."

Because the British were well aware of the Iroquois' need of European goods, they tried to become their sole suppliers of clothing and other necessities so that the Indians would remain loyal to them. In 1776, they successfully cut off the flow of American goods when they defeated American troops led by George Washington in New York City.

British officials also used their friendship with several influential Mohawk leaders to enlist Indian support. Joseph Brant, grandson of one of the Four Indian Kings entertained in London in 1710 and himself a powerful leader and orator, was invited to England. There he heard numerous arguments favoring Iroquois military assistance for Great Britain. Brant returned to New York and spoke vigorously in support of the British cause at council meetings of the confederacy. The league refused to officially endorse either the British or American side. Three nations—the Mohawk, the Seneca, and the Cayuga—favored the British. The Oneida and Tuscarora leaned toward the Americans, and the Onondaga, divided among themselves, were unable to take a stand. Without a consensus, the Iroquois Confederacy adopted a position of neutrality, more by default than by conviction. The dissension among its members shook the stability of the league because the confederacy had always drawn its strength from the principle of unanimity, of One Heart, One Mind, One Law. Reacting to insurmountable disagreements among the nations, confederacy leaders covered up the council fire at the principal Onondaga village in 1777.

Joseph Brant, or Thayendanegea, was an ardent supporter of the British during both the French and Indian and Revolutionary Wars. After the Revolution, Brant secured land for his people near present-day Brantford, Ontario.

This symbolic gesture foreshadowed the end of the league as a dominant political and military force in the region.

Many Mohawk leaders and warriors remained neutral during the Revolution. Others, led by Joseph Brant, supported the British. Several considerations led to their decision. First, after 1776, the British had succeeded in becoming the Mohawks' greatest supplier of tools, clothing, and weapons. The Indians' economic dependence was translated into a military alliance. Second, the Mohawks continued to be wary of colonists' incursions into their territory. They were warned by British officials that a rebel victory would signal the end of the Indians' control over their land. The British argued that the rebels could not be trusted to respect the Mohawks' land claims. Their prediction was supported by an action of the New York legislature during the Revolution. The state claimed all Indian land within its boundaries and promised to give six hundred acres to anyone who enlisted in the rebel army.

Some Mohawks were persuaded to continue their military alliance with Great Britain, while others fought on the side of the Americans. Most, though, remained neutral. Regardless of their allegiances, Mohawk communities around Albany were targets of retaliation by American settlers. Crops were burned, livestock was stolen, and people were attacked. In 1779, an American army under the command of General John Sullivan destroyed Iroquois villages throughout New York.

The Treaty of Paris in 1783 formally concluded the Revolutionary War. It also marked the end of what little security the Mohawks had had in New York. The treaty transferred British territory as far west as the Mississippi River to the victorious Americans. However, it did not address the issue of Indian rights to land in this area. Only Governor Haldimand of Canada spoke up for Indian claims at the treaty conference. He argued that the Natives did not think Great Britain had the right to cede their lands to the United States and wanted to maintain the boundaries provided in the 1768 Treaty of Fort

Stanwix. Haldimand's recommendations were ignored. By the early 1780s, most of the Mohawks had left their traditional lands in New York to seek safety in Canada.

The Mohawk refugees slowly began the process of rebuilding their lives in Canada, hoping finally to live and prosper in peace. They came to reside in five communities—each of which had its own complex history and unique problems and opportunities. The people hoped to be able to reaffirm the ancestral bonds that had kept them of One Mind for so many centuries. But these bonds had been torn asunder by conflicts that the Mohawks did not create but that had, in the end, engulfed them nonetheless.

5

A Nation Divided

M ost of the Mohawks had emigrated from their traditional lands by the end of the eighteenth century and settled in several communities where they hoped to reestablish their lives in tranquility and harmony. The first Mohawk refugees in the seventeenth century wanted to escape from intertribal conflicts caused by economic competition over the *fur trade*. A hundred years later, a new group of refugees left their aboriginal territory because of warfare between Great Britain and the American colonies. In all cases, the Mohawks had to adjust to new circumstances beyond their control. They did so while trying to maintain as much of their traditional culture as possible.

Founded in 1667, the mission settlement of Kahnawake, La Prairie, was located south of Montreal on land granted by the king of France and owned in trust by the Jesuits. Although the majority of Kahnawake's residents were Mohawks, members of other nations in the Iroquois Confederacy sought refuge there as well.

As Kahnawake grew, it became famous for several of its inhabitants. These included a chief known both as Kryn and as Joseph Togouiroui (to-go-wee-RO-wee), who had led a group of forty Catholic Mohawks from New York to Kahnawake in 1673. Another illustrious seventeenth-century resident was a devout woman named Kateri Tekakwitha (ga-de-LEE de-ga-GWEE-ta). Her piety and good works were admired by many of her contemporaries. In recognition of her devotion, Tekakwitha has recently become the first American Indian to be declared by the Catholic Church as venerable and beatified, two steps toward possible sainthood.

The Jesuit missionaries were enthusiastic about the progress of converts at Kahnawake, noting their piety and moral character. In the words of one priest, Father Claude Chauchetiéré, writing in 1694: "Anger is the chief one of their passions, but they are not carried away to excess by it, even in war. Living in common, without disputes, content with little, guiltless of avarice, and assiduous at work, it is impossible to find a people more patient, more hospitable, more affable, more liberal, more moderate in their language."

The community at Kahnawake shifted residence several times in the seventeenth and eighteenth centuries. These moves were necessary because of the depletion of nearby soil, making it unsuitable for planting corn. Kahnawake's present location was established in 1716 on the southern shore of the St. Lawrence River, across from Montreal. The settlement continued to grow. By 1736, an estimated three hundred families resided there.

Living only a few miles from the growing city of Montreal, Kahnawake's inhabitants were under considerable pressure to adopt Canadian mores. Missionaries urged these Mohawks to conform to European standards. The priests instructed married couples to remain together, condemned sexual activity before or outside of marriage, and criticized Mohawk curing practices.

Harmful influences from French settlements sometimes reached Kahnawake. In 1735, Father Luc-François Nau commented: "The Iroquois are more inclined to the practice of virtue than other nations; they are capable of refined feelings but the bad example and solicitations of the French are a very great obstacle to the sanctification of our Iroquois. . . . Taking all into consideration, our Iroquois are much better Christians than the French."

For nearly one hundred years after its founding, the people at Kahnawake often had to choose between allegiance to their kin in New York or to their non-Indian protectors in Quebec. They tried to remain neutral but were continually besieged with requests for aid by both sides. Because of the daily influence of French Jesuits at Kahnawake, the Mohawks there more frequently allied themselves with the French than with their former neighbors. The Kahnawake Mohawks regretted the breach between them and their relatives remaining in New York. French observer Pierre Charlevoix commented that in leaving their ancestral territory, the Mohawks had "abandoned everything that was dearest to them." He added that this was "a sacrifice still more glorious for Indians than for any other nation, because there are none so much attached as they are to their families and their native country."

During the eighteenth century, the Kahnawake Mohawks engaged in the traditional economic tasks of farming, hunting, and fishing. Women planted and harvested their crops. Men left their village for extended periods in autumn and winter to hunt deer and beaver. In addition, the Mohawks raised livestock—such as pigs, poultry, and horses—that had been introduced to North America by Europeans. At Kahnawake, large matrilineal families also lived together in longhouses built in the Iroquoian style. The three Mohawk clans—Bear, Wolf, and Turtle—added to their membership by adopting newcomers from other Indian groups.

Toward the end of the eighteenth century, the fur trade declined in the Northeast because of dwindling supplies of animals. A number of Mohawk men from the villages of Kahnawake and Akwesasne then obtained employment as trappers, loggers, and canoeists with the North West Company, a large fur-trading concern. They headed west across Canada and established a settlement of approximately 250 people in Alberta. Many of these Mohawks remained in Alberta and married into local Indian communities, especially those of the Cree. They were given 25,600 acres of land in Alberta by the Canadian government. (The tract was later reduced to 15,485 acres.) In the 1940s, these lands were expropriated by the province of Alberta. Although their territory was taken away, descendants of this Mohawk group still live in Alberta, British Columbia, and Montana.

In the nineteenth century, men at Kahnawake gradually abandoned hunting. They had less access to forests because of the expansion of Canadian settlements. Farming gained in importance, providing food for residents and produce for sale to neighboring communities. In addition, Mohawk women received income from the sale of handicrafts, such as basketry and beadwork embroidery.

In 1830, the legal status of Kahnawake as a mission settlement changed. The community was reconstituted as a reserve, the Canadian equivalent of a *reservation* in the United States. As a reserve, the land would be held in common by all of its Indian residents and would not be taxed by the Canadian government. As soon as the reserve was established, the Canadian government began to interfere with Mohawk custom by allotting individual homesteads to each male head of household. The traditional composition of Mohawk households, which had always been headed by women, was broken up in an effort to impose the way of life of non-Indian Canadians on the residents of Kahnawake.

The Mohawk mission village of Kanesatake had been built in 1676 on land granted to the Mohawks by Sulpician missionaries on the island of Montreal. After several moves, a

In the late nineteenth century, Mohawk baskets became increasingly popular sparking a cottage industry that took the Akwesasne Mohawks (pictured here) to faraway places such as Lawrence, Kansas, to sell their wares.

permanent settlement was established in 1721 at Lake-of-Two-Mountains, a short distance west of Montreal. The community at Kanesatake, meaning "place of reeds" or "at the foot of the hillside," is sometimes referred to by its Algonkian name Oka (walleyed pike).

In the 1880s, a group of people left Kanesatake and established a small reserve called Wahta (WAH-da), meaning "maple," near Parry Sound, southeast of Georgian Bay in Ontario. This settlement, also called Gibson Reserve, had approximately 250 residents in the nineteenth century.

Sometime between 1747 and 1755, a third settlement of Catholic Mohawks was founded along the St. Lawrence River approximately eighty miles southwest of Montreal. This community—known both as Akwesasne (ah-gwe-SAS-ne), meaning "where the partridge drums," and as St. Regis—was established by people from Kahnawake who had left in search of better soil. The population had grown at Kahnawake, creating a shortage of land and thereby adding another incentive for these people to emigrate. French authorities in Montreal encouraged the new settlement at Akwesasne because they wanted to have another outpost along the St. Lawrence River.

Later, during the American Revolution, the inhabitants of Akwesasne divided into pro-British and pro-American factions. Although most sided with the British, many fought in support of the rebels. A Mohawk leader named Louis Cook (also known as Colonel Louis) was acknowledged by George Washington for his efforts on the Americans' behalf. Washington wrote from Cambridge, Massachusetts, to the Continental Congress in January 1776: "On Sunday evening, thirteen of the [Mohawk] Indians arrived here on a visit. I shall take care that they be so entertained during their stay, that they may return impressed with sentiments of friendship for us, and also of our great strength. One of them is Colonel Louis, who honored me with a visit once before."

After the war, the Treaty of Paris set the boundary between Canada and the United States at 45 degrees north latitude. This line arbitrarily divided Akwesasne into Canadian and American sections. In 1791, New York State sold a large tract of Akwesasne territory to a New Yorker named Alexander Macomb. An area of only six square miles plus two islands in the St. Lawrence were reserved for the Mohawks. They immediately petitioned the state government in Albany, asserting claims to more land. An agreement was finally reached in 1796 that granted the Akwesasne Mohawks two additional tracts of one square mile each along two small rivers. Other portions of their land were sold by New York State in the first half of the nineteenth century, leaving them with fourteen thousand acres in New York and ten thousand acres in Canada. In exchange for these cessions, yearly payments, or annuities, were also guaranteed to the Akwesasne Mohawks.

In the early nineteenth century, the Akwesasne Mohawks were affected by another external war. During the War of 1812 between Great Britain and the United States, authorities in New York prohibited people from Akwesasne to travel outside the reserve unless they secured official passes. This restriction severely limited men's ability to hunt. Even worse, residents were unable to obtain clothing, tools, or other necessary provisions. Indian leaders reacted by requesting supplies from the government. In a letter to Albany, Louis Cook wrote:

> I address you these lines, for the purpose of expressing the situation of my nation, and of giving you assurances of our constantly cherishing good will and friendship towards the United States, and of our determination not to intermeddle with the war which has broken out between them and the English, and which has placed us in so critical a situation. Our young men being prevented from hunting, and obtaining a subsistence for their families, are in want of provisions, and I address myself in their behalf to the justice and liberality of the governor of this state, to obtain a supply of beef, pork and flour, to be delivered to us at St. Regis, during the time that we are compelled to give up our accustomed pursuits.

Cook's request was granted.

Both the British and U.S. governments agreed that Akwesasne should remain neutral in the conflict. However, Akwesasne residents became involved on both sides during the war. Cook joined U.S. forces, as he had during the American Revolution. He was captured by British soldiers in a battle at St. Regis in 1813 and taken to a prison in Quebec, where he died the following year.

After the War of 1812, Canada and the United States began to enforce border restrictions. Before that time, the Akwesasne Mohawks had held their land in common, ignoring the international border. After the war, officials in New York started to issue annuities only to those Indians living on the U.S. side. Canadian authorities barred the New York Mohawks from taking up residence in Canada.

The community was governed locally by two sets of leaders. On the Canadian side, twelve chiefs, selected for life terms, formed an administrative council. These chiefs were chosen from kinship groups in accordance with traditional customs. In New York, a council of three trustees, serving three-year terms, carried out government functions.

People at Akwesasne suffered throughout the nineteenth century from epidemic diseases, especially outbreaks of smallpox, cholera, and typhus. In response to these health crises, New York State opened clinics at Akwesasne in the late nineteenth century. It also gave financial relief, food, and clothing to poor people. Then, in the early twentieth century, New York authorities began an investigation of living conditions on all reservations within the state. Officials undertook this review for two reasons: Medical experts feared that a smallpox epidemic occurring in the Seneca reservations in western New York would spread to neighboring communities. In addition, the state was embroiled in legal battles over Indian land claims. Edward Everett, a state legislator from St. Lawrence County, near the Akwesasne Reservation, was appointed in 1919 to head a commission of inquiry. Everett's panel heard testimony by residents of Iroquois reservations in New York and Canada. In order to determine the legal history of Indian claims, the commissioners reviewed the treaties that the Iroquois had concluded with the United States. Everett based his final report on the second Treaty of Fort Stanwix (1784) in which the federal government transferred title to lands occupied by Indians in New York to the Indians themselves, including the Akwesasne Mohawks. Everett declared: "The passing of the title for this ceded territory to the Indians of this state was a legal and proper transaction. And the

Indians, as a nation, became possessed of the ceded territory." Finally, Everett concluded: "The said Indians of the State of New York, as a nation, are still the owners of the fee simple title to the territory ceded to them by the Treaty of 1784, unless divested of the same by an instrument of equal force and effect as the said treaty of 1784."

In all, Everett declared that New York Iroquois were still owners of six million acres of land in New York. State authorities predictably objected to his conclusions. They refused to consider seriously the facts he presented or to recognize Indian rights. Officials reacted by trying to broaden their control over reservation communities. For instance, in the 1950s, the state extended its jurisdiction over Indian lands in criminal and civil matters.

Within thirty years after the founding of Akwesasne in the eighteenth century, a fourth Mohawk community was established in Canada. The community was settled in 1777 by a group of Mohawks led by Captain John Deserontyon, who had supported the British before and during the American Revolution. The village was located on the north shore of the Bay of Quinté on the northeastern waterways of Lake Ontario. The community was known both as Tyendinega (ti-yen-di-NE-ga), the Mohawk name of Joseph Brant, and as Deseranto, after its founder. Locally, it was administered by a council of eleven hereditary chiefs chosen for life from the eleven matrilineal groups that first settled there.

Many other Mohawks took up residence in a fifth community in Canada, founded just after the end of the American Revolution. This settlement is called Six Nations because its inhabitants were members of all the nations of the Iroquois Confederacy. Six Nations' original residents were either neutral or British-allied Iroquois who sought refuge from American attacks and retaliations taking place in New York. They were led by Joseph Brant, who had always remained loyal to Great Britain. (For additional information on this Mohawk leader, enter "Joseph Brant" into any search engine and browse the many sites listed.)

In 1784, these Indians founded their new community along the Grand River in southern Ontario, a short distance from the U.S. border. The land had been purchased for the Mohawks and their allies by Sir Frederick Haldimand from a group of Indians called the Mississaugas. Haldimand was fulfilling a pledge he made during the war to compensate Indians who fought for England for any losses they suffered as a result of their loyalty. The tract encompassed six miles of land along both sides of the river, totaling 675,000 acres. The population of Six Nations in 1785 consisted of 1,600 Iroquois, including 450 Mohawks, 380 Cayugas, 200 Onondagas, 165 Oneidas, 125 Tuscaroras, and 75 Senecas.

Members of each nation set up a separate village. Like other groups of displaced Mohawks, the people at Six Nations tried to reestablish their culture even though their world had changed forever. As a symbol of determination to assert Iroquois identities and traditions, clan chiefs rekindled the confederacy fire at the Onondaga village at Six Nations. Local government was managed by a council composed of hereditary chiefs from all the nations. Although the six nations were considered equals, Mohawk prominence in the community was evident in that all chiefs spoke the Mohawk language in council deliberations.

Joseph Brant had considerable influence on politics at Six Nations. He believed that the Iroquois should remain strong and sovereign in their new home. He also thought that they needed to adopt some practices of Canadian and American society in order to be economically self-sufficient. Brant urged leaders to sell a large portion of land to Canadian farmers because he hoped that the success of these people would be a good example for the Iroquois. In addition, he wanted to use money received for land to buy food and clothing for indigent Iroquois until they could provide for themselves. After years of debate, some 350,000 acres of land were sold to Canadians, many of whom were friends of Brant's.

Most Iroquois had small farms on which women planted traditional crops using Native farming methods. A few people were able to amass larger holdings. They adopted farming methods introduced by Canadians and grew new crops, such as oats, wheat, and peas. Significantly, these farmers were men, reflecting a shift from the tradition of women being responsible for all farm work.

Throughout the first half of the nineteenth century, farm production gradually increased until many families at Six Nations became fairly prosperous. They produced surpluses, which they sold at markets in nearby cities, such as Brantford and Hamilton, Ontario.

Influences from Canadian society also intensified. Protestant missionaries first built churches at Six Nations in 1827. The Mohawk Institute, a school for Iroquois children, opened in Brantford at about the same time. The first school at Six Nations was constructed in 1831 by Anglican missionaries. Located in the Mohawk community, it offered formal education to all children. In addition, teachers instructed girls in domestic skills and boys in farming techniques. At first, people showed little interest in the schools, but gradually more students enrolled. Missionaries continued to control education at Six Nations until the late 1800s. Many people opposed the schools because they were afraid that exposure to Canadian education would lead to increased *assimilation* and eventual loss of independence. In response to these fears, the Mohawks worked to establish Indian-run schools, and by 1880, thirteen schools were operating.

The people at Six Nations experienced serious health problems in the nineteenth century. They suffered especially from smallpox, measles, and cholera. After a number of years of intermittent medical care, a permanent doctor was employed in 1850 to serve the residents. In 1900, the Six Nations Council established a Board of Health to encourage and coordinate provision of medical services. A tent hospital was opened in 1908. It was replaced in 1927 by the Lady Willingdon Hospital, named after the wife of the Marquess of Willingdon, governor-general of Canada from 1926 to 1931.

As in other Iroquois communities, internal and external pressures to sell additional land continued at Six Nations. Many Indians opposed such sales because they feared losing all their land and their culture. In 1841, the council agreed to turn over Six Nations' land to the British crown to be held in trust. The Canadian government assumed responsibility for evicting non-Indian squatters who had illegally moved onto portions of Six Nations' territory. In the following year, the community was legally formed as a reserve for the Iroquois. Since then, land could only be sold if a majority of the people expressed their approval in a referendum.

Shortly after the reserve was established, the Canadian government began a program of dividing lands into small plots, called *allotments*, which would be owned by individuals. The aim of allotting the reserve was to compel the Iroquois to give up the custom of communal land ownership, which non-Indians saw as an obstacle to the Indians' assimilation into mainstream Canadian society. Between 1847 and 1848, each male head of household was given an allotment of one hundred acres. By 1848, 325 families, consisting of 1,271 individuals, had complied with the program.

The government's policies had far-reaching consequences for Iroquoian culture: First, stressing individual rather than communal ownership of land eroded the Iroquois' unity. Second, land was allotted only to nuclear families—groups made up of a man, a woman, and their children—resulting in the breakup of large extended families that had traditionally been the basis of economic cooperation and interdependence. Third, the program assigned land to men, undermining the roles and rights of women as producers and controllers of food. Not surprisingly, many women resisted the changes because they recognized the danger to their own status. As they feared, women were pressured into giving up productive and public roles in the community. Instead, they became isolated in separate households dominated by their fathers and husbands.

Throughout the second half of the nineteenth century, farming continued to gain importance as a source of food and income from the sale of surpluses. In 1867, the Mohawks founded the Six Nations Agricultural Society, which disseminated techno-logical innovations to the community. It also sponsored annual fairs to showcase the accomplishments of local farmers.

By the early years of the twentieth century, the role of *agriculture* at Six Nations had declined. Small farms were gradually abandoned because they were no longer financially profitable. However, several large farms were quite prosperous. These farms produced various kinds of grains, including corn, oats, and wheat. People also kept livestock, such as dairy and beef cattle, poultry, hogs, and sheep. They sold surplus produce, milk, and animals in nearby Canadian cities.

Unfortunately, these businesses soon began to face financial difficulties. The 1930s—the years of the Great Depression—were especially hard. In order to continue to produce surpluses, Six Nations farmers realized that they needed money to invest in new equipment. But Indians living on reserves had problems obtaining bank loans. Their land was held in trust by the band (the Canadian word for tribe) and therefore could not be used as collateral for a loan. Since the Great Depression, farming has contributed less and less to tribal incomes.

By the late nineteenth century, Mohawk men not engaged in farming were employed in a variety of occupations. They worked at Six Nations or nearby towns and cities as black-smiths, carpenters, builders, and factory laborers.

During this period, conflicts arose over the local form of government. The hereditary chiefs who formed the councils

A rope necklace made from glass beads. Louise McComber, Wolf clan, Kahnawake Reserve.

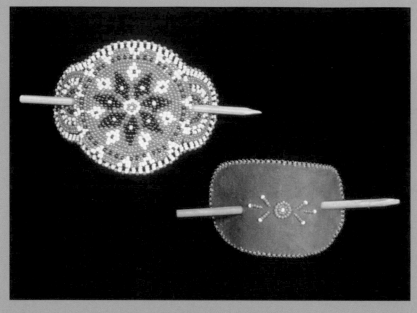

Barrettes made from glass beads and leather. Agnes Decaire, Kahnawake Reserve.

Two cloth whisk-broom holders decorated with floral beadwork designs.
Mary Scott Jacobs, Wolf clan, Kahnawake Reserve.

A glass bead medallion that was woven on a loom. Adeline Etienne, Bear clan, Oka Reserve.

A lidded basket crafted to commemorate the Strawberry Festival held every June at Akwesasne. Christie Arquette, Turtle clan, Akwesasne Reserve.

Mary Adams, a member of the Wolf clan and resident of the Akwesasne Reserve, presented this basket to Pope John Paul II in 1980 when seventeenth-century Mohawk religious figure Kateri Tekakwitha, the "Lily of the Mohawks," was beatified by the Roman Catholic Church.

A multicolor fancy basket woven by Mary Adams, Akwesasne Reserve.

A bandolier bag made from cloth. The beaded design represents the Celestial Tree, which is described in the Mohawks' creation story. David Maracle, Turtle clan, Tyendinega Reserve.

A leather collar adorned with a beaded image of an eagle. Rita Phillips, Wolf clan, Kahnawake Reserve.

Beginning in the late nineteenth century, Mohawk men increasingly partook in occupations such as bridge building (shown here). One such project was the construction of the International Bridge, which connects Sault Ste. Marie, Ontario, and Sault Ste. Marie, Michigan.

tended to be traditionalists. They spoke their native language and opposed the rapid assimilation of Canadian practices. Some were Christians; others followed the traditional religion. These differences often caused rifts within their ranks and made consensus difficult. As a result, some Mohawk Indians began to petition for a change in government. Instead of leadership by hereditary chiefs, they wanted to establish a council of elected representatives. This group called itself the Dehorners, after the traditional method of "dehorning" or impeaching clan chiefs. The Dehorners thought that an elected council would be less divided and more responsive to the people. Others at Six Nations preferred to keep the traditional council. They supported the Iroquois Confederacy and argued that hereditary chiefs symbolized the continuity and sovereignty of the league.

For many years, Canadian authorities refused to mediate the dispute. Then, in 1924, the Canadian Parliament unilaterally dissolved the hereditary system of leadership. The Canadian government wanted to establish an elective system at Six Nations because it believed that such a government would help "modernize" the reserve. The government also knew that hereditary leaders were more likely to fight to hold on to their lands and traditional cultural practices. It called for elections beginning in October 1924.

During the Six Nations Council meeting that September, one month before elections, officers of the Royal Canadian Mounted Police locked the doors to the council chamber during a lunch break while hereditary leaders were absent. The chiefs were thus unable to return to the council hall. Many people, both supporters and opponents of the traditional system, were angered by this display of force. But the elections were held as scheduled. Six electoral districts were set up, each choosing two representatives. In this council of twelve members, each official served for a two-year term. At first, only men could vote in reserve elections. Suffrage was finally extended to women in 1951.

Most residents of the three original mission settlements of Kahnawake, Kanesatake, and Akwesasne were Catholic. Tyendinega and Six Nations were founded by people who followed either the traditional Mohawk religion or various Protestant faiths. However, shortly after these two communities were established in the late eighteenth century, a new religion was introduced on a Seneca reservation in New York. In 1799, a Seneca man named Handsome Lake became deathly ill after years of sickness. During his illness, he received a vision from supernatural messengers instructing him to preach a new faith, or the Good Word, among his people. He recovered and proceeded to make known the message he had received. Known today as the *Handsome Lake Religion* or the Longhouse Religion, the Good Word advises people to return to traditional Iroquoian ethics of cooperation, generosity, and kindness. Many aspects of traditional culture were reinforced by Handsome Lake, including the Four Sacred Rituals and the annual cycle of calendric ceremonies. (For additional information on this religion, enter "Handsome Lake Religion" into any search engine and browse the many sites listed.)

Handsome Lake also stressed the importance of sobriety. His statements against alcohol greatly contributed to his popularity and influence. Handsome Lake was responsible for strengthening the temperance movement not only among the Senecas, Cayugas, and Tuscaroras but also among non-Indians in western New York State.

The religious leader encouraged his people to adopt some Canadian and American practices as well. Among these were non-Indian gender roles and relationships. Handsome Lake favored organizing households of nuclear rather than extended families. He also advocated weakening the bonds between mothers and daughters and strengthening male authority in marital relationships. In addition, he encouraged the use of non-Indian farming methods, especially making farm work the responsibility of men.

Handsome Lake opposed beliefs and practices related to witchcraft. In fact, accusations of witchcraft were often made against prominent women who resisted attempts to curtail their economic and political activities.

The Handsome Lake Religion spread rapidly, first among the Seneca reservations in New York and then to Six Nations in Canada. By the middle of the nineteenth century, followers of Handsome Lake constituted approximately twenty to twenty-five percent of the Six Nations' population, a ratio that remains essentially constant today. The Longhouse Religion was adopted by the Mohawks at Kahnawake in the 1920s and at Akwesasne in the 1930s. Its adherents at both of these reserves constituted a smaller percentage of the population than at Six Nations, but they had great influence on social and political activities.

By the middle of the twentieth century, the people of the various Mohawk communities were adapting to somewhat different local conditions. However, there were also many similarities in their circumstances. All Mohawks had felt pressure to sell lands that had been guaranteed to them forever. Mohawk people from every community often lost out to Canadian and American encroachments but managed to hold on to enough land to assure their survival. They also experienced pressure to assimilate aspects of non-Indian culture. Traditional household groups were disbanded, economic roles were realigned, and native religious beliefs were modified or replaced. But the Mohawks shared much more than these experiences. They were still drawn together by their past and the enduring traditions of the confederacy.

6

Adjusting to Change

In the Mohawk language, the word for Native American is *onkwehonwe* (on-gwe-HON-we), or "real people." Since their first contact with Europeans, the real people have struggled against countless attacks and injustices. All across North America, they have seen their lands diminished, their rights restricted, and their cultures transformed. Many Indian societies were not able to withstand the physical onslaught of foreign armies or the pressure to adapt to foreign cultural practices. But many other Indian peoples have survived and maintained their distinctive values and ways of life. Among these are the Mohawks. Drawing on their past history, the Mohawks in the twentieth century adapted to external conditions, creating their own definition of their place in the modern world.

All Mohawk communities have experienced economic, political, and social changes. Wage work has become the mainstay of Mohawk families. At Six Nations, men and women are employed in businesses and factories in nearby towns and cities. Some men work as mechanics, miners, and builders. Others are employed in automobile factories in Buffalo, New York, and Oakville, Ontario. Women often have jobs as nurses, teachers, factory workers, or service employees.

Many men of Akwesasne and Kahnawake are employed as ironworkers in the construction of bridges and buildings. The Mohawks first became involved in this industry in 1886, when the Dominion Bridge Company negotiated with the Kahnawake Council for access to land through which the firm wished to build a railroad bridge that would stretch across the St. Lawrence River from Montreal to the Quebec mainland near the reserve. In exchange for the use of some reserve land, the company agreed to hire Kahnawake men. After the bridge was completed, many Kahnawake workers helped build the International Bridge that connects Sault Ste. Marie, Ontario, and Sault Ste. Marie, Michigan. Since then, the Mohawk have been attracted to this occupation in large numbers. They have erected bridges and skyscrapers throughout the Northeast. In fact, most Akwesasne and Kahnawake men are employed in high-steel construction for at least some period of their life. These men work in numerous cities, including Buffalo, Rochester, Syracuse, New York, and Boston. They obviously cannot commute to and from their homes and work sites daily, so they reside in city apartments during the week and return to their reserves on the weekend. These men have formed close groups that travel, work, and live together.

Although Mohawk ironworkers usually maintain homes at either Kahnawake or Akwesasne, many families establish residences in cities where the men work. For instance, a sizable Mohawk community grew up in New York City's borough of Brooklyn. During the 1960s and 1970s—the peak years of construction in New York—this community numbered nearly one thousand. As a result of the decline in the availability of work in the 1980s and 1990s, most Mohawk families returned to Kahnawake and Akwesasne. Only about one hundred Mohawks continue to maintain permanent residences in the city.

Because of Kahnawake's location near Montreal, it is one of the most urbanized reserves in Canada. Many people work in Montreal and other Canadian towns and cities close to the reserve. Although Akwesasne is not as urban as Kahnawake, men and women there also work in a wide variety of professional and skilled occupations in nearby Canadian and U.S. locations. The people at Kahnawake and Akwesasne have the highest income per capita of any Canadian reserve.

At the three largest Mohawk reserves—Six Nations, Kahnawake, and Akwesasne—income is generated by employment in band offices, schools, restaurants, stores, and gas stations. Each of these reserves has at least one central village where offices, schools, and stores are located. Ohsweken at Six Nations has a council house, community hall, hospital, police headquarters, post office, and several schools and churches. At Akwesasne, administrative, cultural, and business establishments are located at St. Regis Village in Quebec and at the Community Center, a complex of public buildings near Hogansburg, New York. The village at Kahnawake has band offices, stores, and a hospital.

People living on the three smallest Mohawk reserves—Kanesatake, Tyendinega, and Gibson—have fewer opportunities for employment in their own communities. Some residents of Gibson own cranberry farms on which they produce a large amount of Ontario's supply of this fruit. Most members of these three reserves obtain jobs on nearby farms or in factories and other businesses. For people at all Mohawk reserves, income derived from off-reserve employment is, on average, about 150 percent greater than that obtained from on-reserve work.

In some Mohawk communities, disagreements have grown over questions of leadership and political direction. Governing councils on all the reserves are now chosen through elections. However, this system has a number of problems. Popular involvement in elections is actually quite low. The contests are usually decided by less than one-third of eligible voters.

The low voter turnout is caused, in part, by apathy. More significant, though, is that many people are opposed to an elective system. Instead, they want to reestablish leadership by hereditary chiefs.

Opposition to elective government is often well organized. At Six Nations, many traditionalists have actively sought a change in the system. In 1959, a group of hereditary chiefs, with the help of thirteen hundred supporters, tried to oust the elected council and reinstate themselves as the reserve's official leaders. On March 5, they took over the band council offices, proclaiming the end of the elective system. The chiefs and their followers occupied the council house for one week before being evicted by the Royal Canadian Mounted Police. Even though the occupation ended, dissatisfaction with the elective system continues.

At Kahnawake and Akwesasne, hereditary chiefs are respected members of their communities. Although they do not hold elected office, these leaders wield considerable social and political influence.

One of the most important issues addressed by Mohawk leadership in the last fifty years is the Indians' need and right to own more of their ancestral land. During the 1950s, the governments of Canada and the United States entered into an agreement to construct the St. Lawrence Seaway, a series of locks, dams, and canals along the river that would connect the Atlantic Ocean and the Great Lakes. Since Akwesasne and Kahnawake are located on the shores of the St. Lawrence, this project had an immediate effect on them. The St. Lawrence Seaway Act of 1955 allocated funds for the seaway's construction and granted the two federal governments the right to expropriate land in the project's path. Tracts amounting to 1,260 acres were expropriated at Kahnawake. The Seaway Authority offered monetary compensation, but the band council and many residents refused to surrender their lands.

When the land was taken without their consent, the Kahnawake Mohawks appealed to the United Nations (UN) in 1959, claiming that their human rights, protected by the UN Charter, had been violated. Chief Matthew Lazare petitioned the secretary-general and the Human Rights Commission:

> In violation of treaties between the Six Nations and Britain, and in contradiction to principles of international law, the Canadian authorities have deprived, and continue to deprive, our people of their inherent rights of possession of their land and property by confiscating real and personal property without due process of law and without just, adequate and prompt compensation, in connection with the opening of the St. Lawrence Seaway and other public projects. The method of confiscation is accomplished by brutal force which is unnecessary and unreasonable.

Chief Lazare pointed out that the amount of compensation offered to Indians at Kahnawake and Akwesasne was lower than that extended to non-Indian owners of land along the seaway. Lazare and others hoped that the UN would exert pressure on Canada to "reverse its policy of depriving our sacred Reserve which is the only thing of value left to us, and to refrain from further encroachment on our land and infringement of our rights." Although UN delegates expressed their sympathy to the Kahnawake Council, they took no action to solve the Indians' problem.

In Akwesasne, the St. Lawrence Seaway expropriated eighty-eight acres at Raquette Point, a piece of land on the U.S. side of the reserve that juts out into the St. Lawrence River. The land was removed in order to straighten out the river channel. The Seaway Authority promised a payment of

$100,000, only $31,000 of which has yet been paid. In addition, the authority took Barnhardt Island in the St. Lawrence to build a huge dam. The three-member Akwesasne Council on the U.S. side sued for $34 million in compensation. The New York courts rejected the suit, and in 1959 the U.S. Supreme Court similarly denied their claim. Despite these decisions, the Akwesasne Mohawks have pursued the case. Negotiations are currently under way for a just settlement for Barnhardt Island.

On the Canadian side of Akwesasne, the Seaway Authority expropriated land at Cornwall Island to build an international bridge between Ontario and New York. It expropriated additional acreage there for a Canadian customs station and tollbooths. The customs station and toll collection raised important issues concerning treaty rights. According to Jay's Treaty, a 1794 agreement between Great Britain and the United States, Indians at Akwesasne have the right to cross the border whenever they wish. The Seaway Authority ignored these basic rights by compelling the Akwesasne Mohawks to undergo customs inspections and pay tolls at the international bridge. (For additional information on this treaty, enter "Jay's Treaty" into any search engine and browse the many sites listed.)

After many years of attempting a peaceful mediation of the dispute, the Akwesasne Mohawks blockaded the bridge during the winter of 1969. Only after this action did Canadian authorities finally take notice of the Indians' complaints. They responded by issuing bridge passes to Indians living on the Canadian side of Akwesasne but denied them to those on the U.S. side. The policies enforcing customs inspections were not altered until the 1980s. Now the Akwesasne Mohawks are at last able to exercise the right of free passage that had been guaranteed to them by George Washington and King George III.

Other disputes over land arose at Akwesasne in the 1970s. Akwesasne residents, led by hereditary chiefs and members of the Longhouse Religion, claimed rights to two islands in the

St. Lawrence River in 1970. After a group of Mohawks had occupied the islands for several months, Canadian authorities legally recognized the Akwesasne residents as the owners of the islands.

Three years later, another group of Mohawks, mostly from Akwesasne and Kahnawake, moved onto an unoccupied children's camp at Moss Lake in the Adirondack Mountains of New York. The land was in an area claimed by the Mohawks as part of their original territory that never had been legally sold to New York. After occupying the camp for three years, the Mohawks agreed to exchange this site for state land in nearby Clinton County. They named their new community Ganienkeh (ga-NYEN-ge), meaning "at the flint," and have tried to reestablish many aspects of traditional Mohawk culture there.

In 1970, the New York State Subcommittee on Indian Affairs began an investigation into conditions on Indian reservations, including Akwesasne. Committee members traveled to the reservations and heard testimony from Indian leaders. The panel documented serious problems in education, health, and housing. They recommended more local involvement in planning and staffing programs, more input into developing school curricula reflecting Indian languages and culture, and more funding for housing and health care.

Akwesasne residents have since taken advantage of federal funding available to them to promote bilingual and bicultural education. Several groups have published dictionaries, grammar books, and readers created to help teach children the Mohawk language. Books that recount Mohawk folklore and explain traditional crafts have also been prepared for use at schools attended by Akwesasne children. Most children residing on the U.S. side attend schools in nearby towns; on the Canadian side, however, youngsters are educated at three elementary schools on the reserve. Older students commute to the Canadian city of Cornwall, just across the St. Lawrence River from Cornwall Island.

One Akwesasne leader, Ernest Benedict, founded an innovative educational and cultural program in the 1960s called the Native North American Travelling College (NNATC). Benedict and other activists traveled to reserves throughout Canada to encourage Indian children's awareness of their cultural heritage and help them maintain their traditions. Since the mid-1970s, the NNATC has established a permanent location on Cornwall Island at Akwesasne and greatly expanded its resources. Currently headed by Barbara Barnes, the NNATC is now known as the Ronathahonni Cultural Center and includes a cultural center, library, and museum.

At Six Nations, several organizations encourage learning the traditional languages and cultures of the people. The Woodlands Cultural Centre in Brantford, Ontario, sponsors numerous projects to develop teaching materials and publish books for children and adults.

The health of the people and of the land is another critical problem. At Akwesasne, many farmers noticed damage to their land and animals that they suspected was due to pollution from a nearby Reynolds Aluminum plant. After extensive health surveys by private and public organizations, Reynolds agreed in 1989 to pay $625,000 in compensation to Akwesasne farmers. The General Motors Corporation has also undertaken a cleanup of a toxic dump at their plant near the reservation.

A fundamental issue of concern to the Mohawks in New York and Canada is that of sovereignty—the right to govern one's own nation and control one's destiny. Most leaders strongly believe that Mohawk sovereignty is guaranteed by numerous treaties signed with the United States and Canada. In accordance with these beliefs, leaders of Akwesasne conveyed their thoughts to New York State officials in 1970:

> We are not citizens of state or nation; we have our own nation—the Six Nations. You have no right to legislate for us nor we for you.

WHY OUR CHILDREN SHOULD KNOW THEIR LANGUAGE AND HAVE INDIAN NAMES

Our children must have a name in their native language so the Creator will know them when they pass from this world to the next. All of the Ceremonies must be done in our language as the creator taught us. When no person of our nation speaks our language we will no longer exist as

ONKWEHONWE.

The NNATC or Native North American Travelling College was founded by Ernest Benedict in the late 1960s. The organization's goal is to provide Mohawks with a better understanding of their culture and heritage by traveling to reserves, where they provide educational programs for children. Seen here is an educational poster promoting the study of the Mohawk language.

We are frequently reminded that New York gives us many things. Let us remind you—many Indians work as iron-workers, factory workers, tradesmen. We pay income taxes and gas taxes.

St. Regis reservation was once much larger. Restore it. If we must go through courts you have lost the opportunity to be honorable.

The Mohawk are all one nation, even if some are in Canada.

Both New York State and U.S. federal authorities have been unwilling to grant recognition of total Indian sovereignty and yet have not denied its legitimacy. In one important development on the sovereignty issue, Quebec officials in 1984 signed an agreement with the Kahnawake Council to construct a hospital on the reserve. The wording of this document suggested that the agreement had been made between two legitimate governments. It marked the first time the Canadian government had, in effect, recognized the government of an Indian band as its equal.

New disputes over land and sovereignty continue to arise, however. In the summer of 1990, Oka, a town adjacent to Kanesatake, announced plans to expand a golf course into a wooded area that the town maintained it owned. The Mohawks at Kanesatake claimed that this land belonged to their reserve. In an attempt to stop construction of the golf course, a group from Kanesatake blockaded a road leading to the contested area. Quebec provincial authorities responded by sending police and army troops to confront the protesters. After weeks of negotiations, the Canadian government proposed to pay Oka for the land and transfer it to Kanesatake. Most of the Mohawks agreed to the settlement, and the blockade was lifted. However, some people occupied a community building at Kanesatake for more than two months to bring public attention to the plight of Indian peoples in Canada. When the demonstrators finally left the building, they were arrested and charged with rioting.

Indian groups throughout Canada responded to the conflict at Kanesatake by erecting blockades on their own reserves to show their support of the Mohawks. In British Columbia and Alberta, protesters stopped transportation along several railroad lines. And at Kahnawake, a Mohawk group blockaded the Mercier Bridge that connects Montreal and the southern shore of the St. Lawrence near the reserve.

Another recent controversy at Akwesasne involved the growth of casino gambling on the reserve. The problem began in the 1980s when several Akwesasne residents opened casinos. The traditional Council of Chiefs has steadfastly opposed casinos, which they see as disruptive to their traditional way of life. The elected tribal trustees, however, support residents' rights to operate these establishments.

After simmering for many years, the debate finally erupted during the spring and summer of 1990, when both opponents and supporters erected blockades at several casinos and roads. Troopers from New York and police from Canada occupied Akwesasne for several weeks in July 1990. Although state and provincial police departed soon afterward, tensions decreased only slightly.

The Mohawk Council of Chiefs, supported by the Iroquois Confederacy, appealed to the U.S. government for help. They argued that, according to Jay's Treaty, the federal authorities had an obligation to protect Akwesasne against danger from outside influences. They claimed that because casino gambling was originally a practice of non-Indians, they had a responsibility to prohibit it within reservation boundaries. Other Mohawks still assert that residents have a right to operate these businesses regardless of state or federal regulations. Government officials have not supported either position.

Disagreements among the Mohawks will undoubtedly continue. However, efforts are under way to develop new ways

The Akwesasne Mohawk casino, which opened in 1999, has been a point of contention for Mohawks. The casino has been a good revenue source for the Akwesasne, but the Mohawk community differs on whether or not gaming is an appropriate way to generate income.

to mediate problems and achieve compromises. In October 1990, a committee of the New York State Assembly issued a statement calling into question the state's imposition of an elective system of government at Akwesasne in the nineteenth century. It recommended that this system be abolished and replaced with whatever form of government the community chooses.

7

Mohawks in the Twenty-First Century

As the Mohawks enter the twenty-first century, they face new challenges to their lands and treaty rights, but they also face new opportunities for expanding their sovereignty and improving the lives of their people.

At Kanesatake, the land dispute that erupted over the expansion of a golf course in the town of Oka reached a favorable conclusion for the Mohawk residents. The Canadian government purchased the ninety-two acres of land in dispute from the town of Oka and transferred them to the reserve of Kanesatake. In addition, another agreement was reached in the year 2000 between Kanesatake and the Canadian government. In that agreement, the two parties pledged to negotiate for the eventual transfer of about three thousand acres of land to the reserve. In the interim, the land will be owned by the Canadian government, but it has agreed to transfer the acreage to the full jurisdiction of the Mohawk people.

At the reserve of Kahnawake, located just south of the city of Montreal, officials have been successful in broadening their authority on the reserve and in extending their sovereign powers in relation to the Canadian government. For example, in 1999, the Kahnawake Mohawks signed a series of agreements with the government of Quebec, the province in which their reserve is located. The agreements covered issues of economic development, local justice, and cultural matters. They gave the Mohawks greater authority and control over developing economic projects with partial funding from Quebec. The agreements also gave the reserve the right to establish a local police force and justice system to deal with a range of disputes and criminal behavior.

One of the most important agreements has broad implications for Native sovereignty. It concerns taxation, a critical issue for Native peoples in both Canada and the United States. According to treaties and agreements signed centuries ago between Native leaders and the British, Canadian, and U.S. governments, Native peoples have rights to what is known as "tax immunity"—they are not under the jurisdiction of federal, provincial, or state tax codes. Their land is not subject to property taxes, their earnings (if they work on reserves) are not subject to income taxes, and the purchase of goods on reserves is not subject to sales tax. But throughout the twentieth century, state and federal authorities have tried, bit by bit, to extend tax laws to Indians and to Indian communities. In response, Native governments have attempted to protect their rights to tax immunity. The agreement signed between the Kahnawake Mohawks and the government of Quebec reaffirms the Mohawks' tax-immune status when they purchase goods on the reserve. Most important, it also allows Kahnawake Mohawks to buy goods off the reserve without paying taxes if they present an identification card that registers them as a member of the reserve community.

Kahnawake Mohawks have been vigorous in their commitment to controlling local education for elementary and high school students. They have organized and staffed innovative schools on the reserves that teach children their culture and history in addition to the standard Canadian curriculum. One of the schools teaches young children in their native language in order to ensure the continuation of the Mohawk language and to encourage its use in the community.

Another issue that has stirred debate and continues to do so at Kahnawake is the issue of casino gambling. Many Native communities, both in the United States and Canada, have opened casinos in the hopes of generating income that could revitalize their reserves. Casino gambling is not yet established at Kahnawake but proposals to open casinos have been put forth from time to time. In 1994, a referendum was held on the reserve that asked residents whether they supported or opposed a casino. Opponents of casino gambling narrowly defeated supporters. However, casino supporters have introduced new proposals that, in their opinion, would make a casino more attractive. The operators of the casino would purchase the land from private owners for the building but then the land would become the common property of the reserve as a collective. Additional proposals attempt to counteract the concerns of some people about potential increases in gambling addiction and other antisocial or destructive behavior. According to supporters, the project would include educational outreach services covering gambling and other addictive behavior. Although no decision has yet been reached, it is possible that, sometime in the future, Kahnawake residents will approve the building and operating of a casino on their territory.

The Mohawks at the reserve of Akwesasne are also confronting several important issues in their relationships with neighboring governments, especially with the government of

New York. Taxation has been a point of contention between the tribe and the state for many years. As mentioned earlier, there are no sales taxes collected on products sold on Indian reservations. However, in 1995, New York sought permission from the courts to impose sales taxes on products bought by non-Indians at stores located on Indian reservations in the state. In the same year, the New York Court of Appeals, the state's highest court, ruled that it was legal for the state to collect sales tax on products sold to non-Indians. Reservation governments throughout the state, including the tribe at Akwesasne, objected to this ruling on the grounds that it restricted their sovereignty by permitting the intrusion of state taxation on their territories. Indian owners of stores on the reservations, especially proprietors of small grocery stores and convenience stores, also objected. At least half of the stores' business involves the sale of gasoline and cigarettes to non-Indians who live nearby and take advantage of the lower prices on Indian reservations. New York attempted to begin collecting sales taxes in 1997, but a few months later Governor George Pataki withdrew the order because of opposition from the Mohawks.

However, the issue of taxation on reservations has become a hot topic in New York politics and economics. New York's financial situation deteriorated after the terrorist attacks on New York City on September 11, 2001, which destroyed the World Trade Center and led to a sudden and serious downturn in the stock market. As state revenues declined, officials once again proposed collecting sales taxes on products sold to non-Indians on Indian reservations. In 2003, the state legislature gave the authority to its Department of Taxation and Finance to begin collecting sales taxes on cigarettes and gasoline.

The Mohawks and their tribal leadership object to these proposals on the grounds that the products are purchased on sovereign Mohawk territory. They point out that the state's effort to collect taxes is a violation of their sovereign powers.

The issue is a complex one both legally and economically. It highlights tensions between Native store owners and non-Indian proprietors of convenience stores located off the reservation. The non-Indian store owners claim that the Indians are unfairly attracting customers who would otherwise frequent their establishments. They claim they are losing money because Indian store owners have an advantage in selling non-state-taxed cigarettes and gasoline at lower prices.

For their part, Mohawk store owners claim that they are acting within their legal rights. They also point out that their establishments help neighboring communities because they employ many non-Indian workers in their stores. They say that if their incomes were reduced, they would be forced to lay off many of their workers, resulting in loss of salary and purchasing power. As Barbara Lazore, one of the three Mohawk tribal chiefs, stated: "If we lost revenues for those sales, it would have a devastating effect, not only on our community, but on the North Country economy as a whole." In addition, Lazore pointed out: "We'd have to curtail a lot of programs that people really need, from health to the elderly. It would be devastating. And we wouldn't be the only ones to be hurt. We're one of the biggest employers in the North Country. We employ a lot of non-natives in our community, and many of them would feel themselves suddenly unemployed. Our Native people, too. So, it's not only a Mohawk problem, it's a North Country problem." (For additional information on this Mohawk chief, enter "Barbara Lazore" into any search engine and browse the many sites listed.)

Local officials also fear that the state's efforts to collect taxes might result in confrontations and protests similar to those that happened six years ago when the state first tried to collect sales taxes.

Another issue related to Native sovereignty was settled in 1998. As we've seen, the Akwesasne Reserve is located in two countries, divided by the border between Canada and the

In 2003, Barbara Lazore, a native of Akwesasne, was elected chief to the St. Regis Mohawk Tribal Council. One of three chiefs on the council, she has been fervent in her opposition to the state of New York's attempt to tax Mohawk territory.

United States. For many decades, Mohawks crossing the border from one part of their territory to another had to go through customs inspections. Although Mohawks living in Canada were issued bridge passes that allowed them to cross the border without paying tolls, it was not until the 1980s that separate lanes at the toll stations were set aside for Mohawks so that they would not have to endure routine inspections. Then, in 1998, the Canadian Federal Court of Appeals issued a ruling that was a significant step in promoting Mohawk treaty rights. The ruling confirmed the Mohawks' right to cross the border into Canada with goods that they purchased in the United States. No restrictions were to be applied to their entry into Canada. The goods could be brought into

Canada duty-free and could be intended either for personal use, community use, or for trade with members of other Native nations in Canada.

The Court's ruling is significant in that it establishes rights that in essence respect the sovereignty of the Mohawks. It also begins to address the fact that the Canadian–United States border is an arbitrary international boundary that cuts through the Akwesasne Reserve without the people's consent.

Land claims issues are also continuing to occupy the attention of Mohawk officials and the government of New York. The Mohawk Council of Chiefs filed a land claims suit in New York State courts for approximately 11,600 acres of land as well as several small islands in the St. Lawrence River. According to the claims suit, this land was taken illegally by New York in the nineteenth century. Negotiations between the Mohawks and state officials took place over a period of many years, but in 1996, Governor Pataki broke off talks. Negotiations were later resumed in 2002 with the hopes of reaching a settlement. Then, in 2003, the elected tribal chiefs of the Akwesasne Mohawks and Governor Pataki signed a "memorandum of understanding" to end the dispute. Although this was welcome news, it was complicated by the fact that the memorandum ties the settlement of the land claims case to the issue of casino gambling. According to the agreement, the Mohawk tribe would receive $100,000,000 from the state in order to buy about 7,000 acres of land in areas near the reservation. Current landowners will not be forced to sell their land to the Mohawks but, if they are willing, the land will be purchased and become part of the Akwesasne Reservation.

As part of the agreement, the Akwesasne Mohawks would be permitted by the state to construct and operate a gaming casino in the Catskill Mountains of southern New York even though that location is not now part of or adjacent to Mohawk territory. Another item in the memorandum permits the Mohawks to install and operate slot machines at the casino that has been operating on their reserve since 1993. Revenues collected from the slot machines will be divided between the tribe and the state. During the first three years of operation, one-fifth of the income will go to the state. Beginning in the fourth year, one-quarter of the revenue will go to the state.

While this agreement was hailed by some as a breakthrough in the land claims dispute, other members of the Akwesasne community objected to the fact that the tribe would only acquire a portion of the original 11,600-acre territory in dispute. The tribe would essentially be abandoning its claim to more than 4,000 acres of land. The agreement does call for a referendum in the Akwesasne community so that tribal members can voice their approval or rejection. The referendum has not yet taken place but opponents held protests to voice their objections.

Regularly scheduled elections took place for members of the Tribal Council in June 2003. All candidates except the incumbents were opposed to the memorandum, so the election in effect functioned as an unofficial referendum. None of the incumbents were reelected. Instead they were replaced by members who were opposed to the memorandum. Then, in October 2003, the new Tribal Council wrote a letter to Governor Pataki, officially stating their intention to withdraw from the memorandum of agreement. They said they believe that the issues combined in the document should be separated. The issues of taxation, land claims, and casino gaming are each critical and complex problems that need to be worked out separately.

Even the casino located on Akwesasne territory that opened in 1993 is embroiled in controversy. In addition to differences of opinion within the Mohawk community about whether or not a casino is an appropriate way to generate income, the New York State courts have now entered the picture. Before the casino opened, the Akwesasne Mohawks negotiated a compact with the state that enabled the Indians to operate the casino.

However, the compact was neither approved nor rejected by the state legislature. Then, in 2003, the New York State Court of Appeals ruled that the compact was invalid because the state legislature had never acted on it. The court did allow the casino to remain open pending action by the legislature.

The issue of casino gambling on Mohawk reservations, and indeed throughout the United States, raises complex issues within reservation communities and elsewhere in their regions. Indian communities often want to operate casinos as a way to generate necessary income. The Akwesasne Reservation is located in a rural part of New York where it is difficult to attract manufacturers or other businesses that could employ larger numbers of people. The Mohawks, like other Native Americans, look to casino gaming to employ their residents and to attract visitors who spend money not only at the casinos but at restaurants, stores, and hotels in the area. In fact, most Indian casinos generate more income for non-Natives than they do for members of the reservation. For this reason, many non-Native communities near reservations benefit from their proximity to Indian casinos. They obtain jobs at the casinos, their stores and hotels attract customers, and the state receives revenues from agreements that give them a percentage of the casino's earnings.

The Akwesasne community has made significant strides in establishing educational programs and health programs on the reservation to meet the needs of its residents. They have a network of services to deliver health care to the elderly and homebound, and they have established educational programs for young children, teaching the Mohawk language and stressing traditional beliefs and practices. Mohawk children are learning the history and culture of their people.

Economic statistics gathered by the U.S. Census in 2000 for the U.S. portion of Akwesasne indicate continuing economic problems. The per-capita income for residents of the reservation was $12,017, while the median family income was $34,336. These numbers are substantially below the norm for their New York neighbors. The state per-capita income stood at $32,108, while the median family income was $36,369. Akwesasne residents are even worse off when compared to the nationwide averages. The United States per-capita income in 1998 was $27,203 and median family income stood at $46,737.

The low level of income at Akwesasne is reflected in relatively high rates of poverty. In 1999, about 19.4 percent of the families at Akwesasne were living below the poverty level. For families with children under five years of age, the poverty rate was even higher, standing at 33.5 percent. The poverty rate for individuals on the reservation was 22.4 percent. These figures compare unfavorably to the poverty rate of 16.7 percent for individuals in New York and to the U.S. national poverty rate of 12.7 percent. Poverty rates, then, for the Mohawks are substantially higher than those for New Yorkers and Americans in general.

Data on employment reveal that 65 percent of Akwesasne residents report working in the civilian labor force. Of the residents, 60.2 percent are employed, while 4.8 percent are unemployed. The unemployment figure is probably inaccurate because 35 percent of the people are "not in the labor force." Some of those not in the labor force may be elderly people who have retired or women who are stay-at-home moms but some have been unemployed for a long time and no longer actively seek work because they have no hope of obtaining jobs. In any case, Akwesasne data reveal higher rates of unemployment than national figures. In the United States, 67.1 percent of the population reported being employed, 32.9 percent were "not in the labor force," and 4.2 percent were unemployed.

Additional data contained in the 2000 Census reveal interesting aspects of the Akwesasne community. Of the 2,699 people living on the reserve (on the U.S. side), 97.7 percent are Native American while 2.1 percent are white. The median age of reservation residents is 30.3 years, somewhat higher than other reservations but significantly lower than the U.S. median age of 35. The average size of families is 3.44 persons, a figure somewhat lower than other Native families living on reservations but considerably higher than the U.S. median family size of 2.61 persons. When taken together, these age and family statistics indicate that Mohawk families consist of a larger number of children than do average American families.

Data on education reveal that members of the Mohawk community at Akwesasne peform about as well as the average for Indian reservations in the United States. At Akwesasne, 67.5 percent of adults aged 25 or over are high school graduates. In addition, 7.7 percent are college graduates or have obtained a higher degree.

The census statistics reveal that a vast majority of Mohawk people living at Akwesasne are monolingual speakers of English. That is, 90.2 percent of residents aged five years and over speak English only. The remaining 9.8 percent speak Mohawk in addition to English. A smaller number, 0.5 percent, report that they speak English less than "very well." These data reveal that the Mohawk language has an uncertain future in the community. The fact that nearly 10 percent of residents are speakers of the language might indicate that the language will be passed down to future generations. But the small percentage also indicates that efforts must be made to guarantee its future. It is imperative that the language continues to be taught to young children so that when they grow up they can in turn teach it to their children and grandchildren.

The largest of the Mohawk reserves is the one at Akwesasne. Combining figures from the 2000 U.S. Census Bureau and Canadian statistics, the reserve had 10,680 residents in the year 2000. An additional 1,788 people were members of the Akwesasne Band but did not live on the reservation. Next in size is the reserve at Kahnawake. It had 7,225 residents. The Iroquois reserve of Six Nations, located a short distance north of Buffalo, New York, in southern Ontario, has residents of all six Iroquois peoples (Mohawks, Oneidas, Onondagas, Cayugas, Senecas, and Tuscaroras). The Mohawk population at Six Nations numbers 5,013. Another Mohawk reserve, called Tyendinega, located on the northern shore of Lake Ontario, has a resident population of 1,944. Finally, the small reserve of Kanesatake, located a short distance west of Montreal near the town of Oka, has 1,358 residents.

These figures document the number of people residing on the reserves. But Canadian government statistics also report the number of people who are members of First Nations but who do not live on their reserves. The table below displays the data for resident and non-resident Band members.

RESERVATION	RESIDENT POPULATION	MEMBERS LIVING OFF RESERVE	TOTAL*
Akwesasne	10,680	1,788	12,468
Kahnawake	7,225	1,861	9,092
Six Nations	5,013	5,029	10,042
Tyendinega	1,944	5,325	7,270
Kanesatake	1,358	631	1,990

*Note that the total figures may be more than the resident population plus the off-reserve population because a small number of people live on "Crown Land," public land that is not part of the reserve.

Much has changed for the Mohawks over the centuries. Most likely, the people at Akwesasne, Kahnawake, Kanesatake, Six Nations, and Tyendinega will probably not be able to create a government and a community based wholly on the principles of the ancient Confederacy: to be of One Heart, One Mind,

One Law. However, they are committed to protect their sovereignty, secure their rights, and live in the way that best suits their aspirations. Knowledge of their history and satisfaction with their past and present achievements will no doubt keep alive their pride in being the People of the Place of Flint, the respected Keepers of the Eastern Door.

The Mohawks at a Glance

Tribe	Mohawk
Culture Area	Northeast
Original Geography	Eastern New York and western New England; Mohawk and Hudson River valleys
Linguistic Family	Iroquoian
Current Population (2000)	Approximately 40,000
First European Contact	Samuel de Champlain, French, 1609
Federal Status	Native bands in Canada: Akwesasne, Kahnawake, Kanesatake, Tyendinega, Six Nations; tribal reservation in New York: Akwesasne

1700 B.C. – 1200 B.C. Ancestors of the Mohawks and other Iroquoian peoples migrate from the west and settled in the northeastern United States.

A.D. 1300 Development of Iroquois culture, Late Woodland Cultural Tradition.

1300s – 1400s Founding of the Iroquois Confederacy, consisting of the Mohawks, Oneidas, Onondagas, Cayugas, and Senecas.

Early 1600s Establishment of trade with the Dutch along the Hudson River.

1609 Mohawks attacked near what is now Lake Champlain by a group of Hurons, Algonkians, and French, led by Samuel de Champlain.

1615 Dutch establish trading posts at Fort Orange (later called Albany).

1653 Mohawks sign treaty of peace and friendship with the French.

1664 Dutch are defeated by Great Britain; British take Fort Orange, rename it Albany.

1667 Mohawk converts to Catholicism are persuaded to leave their villages and settle at a French Jesuit mission near Montreal, later moved to Kahnawake.

1676 Mohawk mission village established west of Montreal, called Kanesatake.

1747 – 1755 Mohawk community founded along St. Lawrence River, eighty miles southwest of Montreal; called Akwesasne by former residents of Kahnawake.

1754 – 1763 French and Indian War (called the Seven Years' War in Europe) is fought.

1768 Mohawks sign treaty of Fort Stanwix with Great Britain, guaranteeing the safety of their land and borders.

1775–1783 American Revolution, in which the Mohawks side with the unsuccessful British, is fought.

1777 Chiefs of the Iroquois Confederacy cover up the council fire at Onondaga because of disagreements over whether to take sides during the Revolutionary War; Mohawk community founded north of Lake Ontario, called Tyendinega.

1779 George Washington sends an army led by General John Sullivan to destroy Iroquois villages in New York.

1784 Members of the Mohawk and other Iroquois nations found the Six Nations Reserve near Brantford, Ontario.

1794 Signing of Jay's Treaty between the United States and Great Britain, guaranteeing the right of Native peoples to freely cross the border between the United States and Canada.

1799 The beginning of the Handsome Lake Religion among the Senecas; later spread to all Iroquois nations.

1824 Bureau of Indian Affairs established.

1827 Protestant missionaries first build churches at Six Nations.

1830 Kahnawake reconstituted from a mission settlement to a reserve by the Canadian government.

1841 Six Nations Council agrees to turn over its land to the British crown to be held in trust.

1861–1865 American Civil War.

1867 Mohawks found the Six Nations Agricultural Society.

1880 Founding of the Mohawk community called Wahda in Ontario.

1886 Dominion Bridge Company negotiates with the Kahnawake Council for access to land through which the firm wishes to build a railroad bridge that would stretch across the St. Lawrence River from Montreal to the Quebec mainland near the reserve.

1924   The U.S. government grants citizenship rights to all Native Americans.

1924   Canadian Parliament unilaterally dissolves system of hereditary leadership on Indian reserves in Canada.

1955   Passage of the St. Lawrence Seaway Act that legislates an agreement between the United States and Canada to build the St. Lawrence Seaway, eventually appropriating land from the Akwesasne and Kahnawake Reserves.

1984   The first government-to-government agreement between Canada and a Mohawk Reserve: Canadian officials and leaders of the Kahnawake Reserve sign an agreement to construct a hospital on the reserve; Canadian government recognizes the government of an Indian band as its equal.

1987   U.S. Supreme Court rules that if a state permits any type of gambling, then Indian casinos there were legal; Congress passes the Indian Gaming Regulatory Act the following year.

1990   Canadian Federal Court of Appeals issues a ruling confirming the right of Mohawk people to cross the border into Canada with goods that they purchased in the United States, reconfirming provisions of the 1794 Jay's Treaty.

2003   Signing of a "memorandum of understanding" between the tribal chiefs of the Akwesasne Mohawks and New York Governor George Pataki to settle a land claim case for about 11,600 acres of land, illegally taken by New York in the nineteenth century.

agent—A person appointed by the Bureau of Indian Affairs to supervise U.S. government programs on a reservation and/or in a specific region.

agriculture—Intensive cultivation of tracts of land, sometimes using draft animals and heavy plowing equipment. Agriculture requires people to live in fairly permanent settlements.

Algonkians—The Indian peoples living in the northeastern United States and east-central Canada whose languages are related and who share numerous cultural characteristics.

Algonquian—The languages spoken by most Indian peoples in northeastern North America, including those who were geographically closest to the Iroquois.

allotment—U.S. policy applied nationwide through the General Allotment Act of 1887, aimed at breaking up tribally owned reservations by assigning individual farms and ranches to Indians. Allotment was intended as much to discourage traditional communal activities as to encourage private farming and assimilate Indians into mainstream American life.

assimilation—The complete absorption of one group into another group's cultural tradition.

Bureau of Indian Affairs (BIA)—A U.S. government agency now within the Department of the Interior. Originally intended to manage trade and other relations with Indians, the BIA today seeks to develop and implement programs that encourage Indians to manage their own affairs and to improve their educational opportunities and general social and economic well-being.

clan—A multigenerational group having a shared identity, organization, and property based on belief in their descent from a common ancestor. Because clan members consider themselves closely related, marriage within a clan is strictly prohibited.

confederacy—A union of related tribes or nations that functions as a political, military, and/or economic unit.

culture—The learned behavior of humans; nonbiological, socially taught activities; the way of life of a group of people.

fur trade—Trading network in North America through which Indians gave Europeans animal pelts in exchange for manufactured goods.

Handsome Lake Religion—A religious movement (also known as the Longhouse Religion and the Good Word) founded in 1799 by a Seneca man named Handsome Lake. This faith encouraged a return to traditional Iroquoian ways.

Iroquoian—A large group of separate tribal peoples in the Northeast and Carolina regions speaking related languages and having similar cultures. Most were eventually conquered or incorporated by the Six Nations. Also, the languages spoken by these tribal groups.

Iroquois—The members of a confederacy of Iroquoian peoples. Founded in about 1500, the Iroquois Confederacy originally included the Mohawk, Oneida, Onondaga, Cayuga, and Seneca tribes. The Tuscarora joined the Iroquois League in 1722.

Jesuit—A member of the Society of Jesus, a Roman Catholic order founded by Saint Ignatius of Loyola in 1534. The Jesuits are highly learned and, in the seventeenth century, were particularly active in spreading Christianity outside Europe.

lineage—A group of individuals related through descent from a common ancestor; a descent group whose members recognize as relatives people on the mother's side only or the father's side only.

longhouse—A structure with a frame made of cedar covered with bark and branches in which most Iroquoian peoples, including the Mohawks, lived. These dwellings were up to two hundred feet long and could house ten or twelve families.

matrilineal—Descent rules for determining family or clan membership by tracing kinship through female ancestors.

mission—A religious center founded by advocates of a particular denomination who are trying to convert nonbelievers to their faith.

missionaries—Advocates of a particular religion who travel to convert nonbelievers to their faith.

moiety—A grouping of clans. The Mohawk Nation was divided into two moieties.

nation—A term used generally by the early Europeans in North America to describe the Indian tribal societies they encountered. Broadly, any large group of people having similar institutions, language, customs, and political and social ties.

removal policy—A federal policy of the early nineteenth century that called for the sale of all Indian land in the eastern United States and the migration of Indians from these areas to lands west of the Mississippi River.

reservation, reserve—A tract of land retained by Indians for their own occupation and use. *Reservation* is used to describe such lands in the United States; *reserve*, in Canada.

treaty—A contract negotiated between representatives of the U.S. government or another national government and one or more Indian tribes. Treaties dealt with the cessation of military action, the surrender of political independence, the establishment of boundaries, terms of land sales, and related matters.

tribe—A society consisting of several or many separate communities united by kinship, culture, language, and other social institutions including clans, religious organizations, and warrior societies.

wampum—Shell beads used by tribes in the northeastern United States in strings or belts as a pledge of the truth of their words, symbols of high office, records of diplomatic negotiations and treaties, and records of other important events.

Books

Colden, Cadwallader. *The History of the Five Indian Nations.* 1727. Reprint. Ithaca, N.Y.: Cornell University Press, 1958.

Ghobashy, Omar. *The Caughnawaga Indians and the St. Lawrence Seaway.* New York: Devin-Adair, 1961.

Grinde, Donald, and Bruce Johansen. *Ego Aside of Native America: Environmental Destruction of the Indian lands and Peoples.* Santa Fe, N.M.: Clear Light Publishers, 1995.

Hertzberg, Hazel. *The Great Tree and the Longhouse.* New York: Macmillan, 1966.

Landsman, Gail. *Sovereignty and Symbol: Indian-White Conflict at Ganienkeh.* Albuquerque, N.M.: University of New Mexico Press, 1988.

Morgan, Lewis. *League of the Iroquois.* 1851. Reprint. New York: Corinth Books, 1962.

Parker, A.C. The Constitution of the Five Nations. New York State Museum Bulletin #184, 1916.

Shimony, Annemarie. *Conservatism among the Iroquois at the Six Nations Reserve.* New Haven, Conn.: Yale University Press, 1961.

Tehanetorens. *Tales of the Iroquois.* Rooseveltown, N.Y.: *Akwesasne Notes*, 1976.

Trigger, Bruce, ed. *The Handbook of North American Indians.* Vol. 15, *The Northeast.* Washington, D.C.: Smithsonian Institution, 1978.

Wilson, Edmund, and Joseph Mitchell. *Apologies to the Iroquois: With a Study of the Mohawks in High Street.* New York: Vintage Books, 1959.

Websites

The Mohawk Nation Home Page
http://www.peacetree.com/akwesasne/home.htm

Official Webpage of Akwesasne Mohawk Nation
http://www.akwesasne.ca

Official Website of the Mohawk Council of Kahnawake
http://www.kahnawake.com

Website of the Kanesatake Mohawk
http://www.kanesatake.com

page:
3: © Hulton|Archive
by Getty Images
7: National Museums of Canada
11: © G.E. Kiddder Smith/
CORBIS
26: Library of Congress
29: Library of Congress
32: Library of Congress
37: Library of Congress
49: National Archives of Canada
55: Library of Congress

62: Library of Congress
71: The Kanieh'Kehaka Raotitiohkwa
Cultural Center
83: The Ronathahonni
Cultural Center
86: Associated Press, AP/
Michael Okoniewski
92: Courtesy of Public Information
Office, St. Regis Mohawk Tribe
A-I: Iroquois Indian Museum,
Howes Cave, N.Y.

Cover: Iroquois Indian Museum, Howes Cave, N.Y.

Nancy Bonvillain, Ph.D., is currently a visiting faculty member in the summer session at Columbia University and teaches anthropology and linguistics at Simon's Rock College of Bard in Great Barrington, Massachusetts. She has written more than a dozen books, including volumes in Chelsea House's INDIANS OF NORTH AMERICA series (*The Huron, Mohawk, Hopi, Teton Sioux, Haida, Sac* and *Fox, Inuit, Zuni, Santee Sioux, Native American Religion* and *Native American Medicine*). And she has written two volumes of Native American biographies, *Hiawatha* and *Black Hawk*, in the NORTH AMERICAN INDIANS OF ACHIEVEMENT series.

Dr. Bonvillain's concentrations within the field have been in Native American studies and in linguistics. She has carried out fieldwork in the Navajo Nation in Arizona and the Akwesasne Mohawk Reserve located in Ontario/Quebec and New York. Her dissertation was a study of the Mohawk language as spoken at the Akwesasne Reserve. She has also prepared a Mohawk/English dictionary and book of conversations for use at the schools on the reserve.

Ada E. Deer is the director of the American Indian Studies program at the University of Wisconsin-Madison. She was the first woman to serve as chair of her tribe, the Menominee Nation, the first woman to head the Bureau of Indian Affairs in the U.S. Department of the Interior, and the first American Indian woman to run for Congress and secretary of state of Wisconsin. Deer has also chaired the Native American Rights Fund, coordinated workshops to train American Indian women as leaders, and championed Indian participation in the Peace Corps. She holds degrees in social work from Wisconsin and Columbia.